W O R K B O O K

BASIC GRAMMAR IN MANY VOICES

Marilyn N. Silva

California State University, Hayward

Prepared by Robert Mann

NTC Publishing Group
a division of NTC/CONTEMPORARY PUBLISHING COMPANY
Lincolnwood, Illinois USA

ISBN: 0-8442-5956-X (student workbook)
ISBN: 0-8442-5956-0 (answer key)

Published by NTC Publishing Group,
a division of NTC/Contemporary Publishing Company,
4255 West Touhy Avenue,
Lincolnwood (Chicago), Illinois 60646-1975 U.S.A.
© 1998 NTC/Contemporary Publishing Company
7 8 9 0 ML 0 9 8 7 6 5 4 3 2 1

CONTENTS

P R E F A C E

For every exercise in *Basic Grammar in Many Voices* there are three additional exercises in the *Workbook*. These exercises provide additional practice for concepts or skills that you may find difficult. If you find that any of these exercises stump you, go back to *Basic Grammar in Many Voices* and reread the related material.

CHAPTER ONE

Recognizing Nouns and Pronouns

Exercise 1.1(a) Using Articles to Identify Nouns

In the following sentences from *Travels with Charley* by John Steinbeck, circle every article you find and underline the noun that it introduces.

1. The night was loaded with omens.

2. He collected directly from the farmers.

3. On the bed beside me I had a flashlight.

4. The beer came in a can.

5. Charley didn't bark an alarm, but he growled and whined uneasily.

6. It seemed hours since I had passed a car or a house or a store.

7. The darkness crept down.

8. The men turned her around like a doll.

9. There was a knock on the door.

10. I have been told that the crop is harvested by Canucks from Canada.

Exercise 1.1(b) Using Articles to Identify Nouns

In the following sentences from *Black Boy* by Richard Wright, circle every article you find and underline the noun that it introduces.

1. I picked up the money and did not count it.

2. I ran out of the kitchen and into the backyard.

3. Yes, there was really a fire.

4. Shuddering, I fumbled at the rope and the kitten dropped to the pavement with a thud that echoed in my mind for many days and nights.

5. The food was kept hot on the stove.

6. In the end I was so angry that I refused to talk about the story.

7. Steeped in new moods and ideas, I bought a ream of paper and tried to write.

8. The loss of my job did not evoke in me any hostility toward the system of rules.

9. I went into the kitchen.

10. I ached to be of an age to take care of myself.

Exercise 1.1(c) Using Articles to Identify Nouns

In the following sentences from *Jazz* by Toni Morrison, circle every article you find and underline the noun that it introduces.

1. The sun sneaks into the alley behind them.

2. The thump could not have been a raccoon.

3. Finally she decided to mail it with a note of her own attached—urging caution and directing daddy's attention to a clipping from *Opportunity Magazine*.

4. The singer is hard to miss.

5. I had to sneak a look at her.

6. Her brother-in-law was not a veteran, and he had been living in East St. Louis since before the War.

7. I have seen her, passing a café or an uncurtained window.

8. The children ate the chocolate from the ingots of gold.

9. People neither of them has seen before join the fun as easily as those who have grown up in the building.

10. The argument had been too good.

Exercise 1.2 (a) Noun Phrases and Adjectives

Underline the noun phrases introduced by articles in the following sentences from *Travels with Charley.* Circle the adjectives you find in the noun phrases you underline.

1. He was a small boy.

2. We brought out a radio for reports, since the power would go off if Donna struck.

3. The overloaded springs sighed and settled lower and lower.

4. A light anchor went down and they were left.

5. If I were a good businessman, I would gather all the junk and the wrecked automobiles.

6. I banged the little bell on the desk, then called out, "Anybody here?"

7. I remember as a child reading or hearing the words "The Great Divide" and being stunned by the glorious sound, a proper sound for the granite backbone of a continent.

8. A great gothic wood stove clicked and purred.

9. We were to eat at a square table.

10. Mount Toro was a rounded benign mountain, and to the north Monterey Bay shone like a blue platter.

© 1998 NTC/Contemporary Publishing Co.

Exercise 1.2 (b) Noun Phrases and Adjectives

Underline the noun phrases introduced by articles in the following sentences from *Black Boy*. Circle the adjectives you find in the noun phrases you underline.

1. I was overwhelmed by the faces and the voices which I could not understand.

2. High above me was a white face which my mother told me was the face of the judge.

3. I sat down amid a profound silence.

4. The home did not have the money to check the growth of the wide stretches of grass by having it mown, so it had to be pulled by hand.

5. Each new school meant a new area of life to be conquered.

6. I forgave him and pitied him as my eyes looked past him to the unpainted wooden shack.

7. There was the suspense I felt when I heard the taut, sharp song of a yellow-black bee hovering nervously but patiently above a white rose.

8. A wide dusty road ran past the house.

9. I grabbed the sides of the buggy, ready to jump, even though I could not swim.

10. One of the strange, striped animals turned a black face upon me.

Exercise 1.2 (c) Noun Phrases and Adjectives

Underline the noun phrases introduced by articles in the following sentences from *Jazz*. Circle the adjectives you find in the noun phrases you underline.

1. The best thing to find out what's going on is to watch how people maneuver themselves in the streets.

2. The dark rooms grow darker: the parlor needs a struck match to see the face.

3. The slush at the curb is freezing again.

4. And even though the confirmation would shame him, it would make him the happiest boy in Virginia.

5. The old father didn't know a thing.

6. Chief among them was fear and—a new thing—anger.

7. Alice waited this time, in the month of March, for the woman with the knife.

8. It bounced off, making a little dent under her earlobe, like a fold in the skin that was hardly a disfigurement at all.

9. Sitting in the thin sharp light of the drugstore playing with a long spoon in a tall glass made her think of another woman occupying herself at a table pretending to drink from a cup.

10. Following her gaze Alice lifted the iron and saw what Violet saw: the black and smoking ship burned clear through the yoke.

Exercise 1.3 (a) Determiners

Circle each determiner you encounter in the following sentences from Willa Cather's *The Professor's House*. Then underline the noun phrase it begins, including any adjectives that may come between the determiner and the noun.

1. Lillian held up lovingly in her fingers a green-gold necklace.

2. He sat down, and Marsellus brought him some tea, lingering beside his chair.

3. He walked up to the chair where his wife was reading, and took her hand.

4. She was gone a great while—perhaps ten actual minutes.

5. But they would go to any amount of trouble and no inconsiderable expense to save him a few thousand francs.

6. She was intensely interested in the success and happiness of these two young men.

7. Science hasn't given us any new amazements.

8. Most of his colleagues were much older than he, but they were not his equals either in scholarship or in experience of the world.

9. Her upper lip had grown longer.

10. This room had been his center of operations.

Exercise 1.3 (b) Determiners

Circle each determiner you encounter in the following sentences from Thomas Sanchez's *Rabbit Boss*. Then underline the noun phrase it begins, including any adjectives that may come between the determiner and the noun.

1. The men outside were shouting, their voices booming out across the flatness of the Big Lake in celebration.

2. With each step his boots smacked hard on the packed snow.

3. Captain Rex saw the gloved hand, the white broadcloth coat, just slightly frayed at the cuff.

4. Two men struggled the large barrel off the back of the wagon.

5. There's your cannibals for you, cannibals in tailored sharkskin suits.

6. The smooth balloon of his face which floated up off his short body always had a cheery-delicate smile painted on it.

7. Behind him the march broke out on two sides.

8. There was one girl that a man had to stand in line to dance with.

9. For four nights the Man of Medicine came and the people waited outside.

10. The spider clung to its essence.

© 1998 NTC/Contemporary Publishing Co.

Exercise 1.3(c) Determiners

Circle each determiner you encounter in the following sentences from Kurt Vonnegut's *Bluebeard*. Then underline the noun phrase it begins, including any adjectives that may come between the determiner and the noun.

1. The Bluebeard story notwithstanding, there are no bodies in my barn.

2. Dorothy remarried soon after our divorce, remarried happily, from all accounts.

3. I was becoming a man, and didn't need a mother anymore, or so I thought.

4. The first person I told about this magnificent opportunity was the editor.

5. That story, incidentally, was made into the movie *You're Fired*, the second movie to star sound as well as images.

6. I have just given this quiz to Celeste and her friends.

7. That higher civilization doesn't have to be another country.

8. The old gentleman sat back, seemingly much pleased by this answer.

9. I had no friends.

10. My father was going to be buried wearing a pair of his own cowboy boots.

Exercise 1.4 (a) Compound Nouns

Each of the following sentences from *Breathing Lessons* by Anne Tyler has at least one compound noun. Underline every compound noun you find.

1. Also their car was in the body shop.

2. Maybe she would hire on as a crossing guard when Leroy started school.

3. She passed the first of the ranch houses.

4. The plaid-shirt boys, the gym-sneaker boys: Those were the ones she'd gravitated toward.

5. I was her official labor coach.

6. She wore a pink tank top with some kind of red stain down the front.

7. The coffee table bore sliding stacks of magazines and comic books.

8. She was carrying two cans and a sack of potato chips.

9. Maggie started collecting soft-drink lids from the floor of the car.

10. Things had been allowed to just happen—a barbecue joint sprouting here, a swim-pool display room there.

Exercise 1.4 (b) Compound Nouns

Each of the following sentences from *Song of Solomon* by Toni Morrison has at least one compound noun. Underline every compound noun you find.

1. Reba was scratching out tiny flowers with a nail file.

2. Pilate stood up, wrapped her quilt around her, and with a last fond look at the baby, left through the kitchen door.

3. When Macon walked out of the yard, the sun had disappeared behind the bread company.

4. Collecting his father's rents gave him time to visit the wine house.

5. Guitar paid their bar bill.

6. She gave up, apparently, all interest in table manners or hygiene, but acquired a deep concern for and about human relationships.

7. Obviously she could not put up the screens, take down the storm windows, or endure any sustained heavy cleaning.

8. She put her hand on the door handle and found it locked.

9. He stopped and began to move slowly sideways, the branch tip scratching a yard or so ahead.

10. Milkman followed his finger, and hobbled over the gravel and ties to the station house.

Exercise 1.4 (c) Compound Nouns

Each of the following sentences from *The Crying of Lot 49* by Thomas Pynchon has at least one compound noun. Underline every compound noun you find.

1. The letter was from the law firm of Warpe, Wistfull, Kubitschek and McMingus, of Los Angeles.

2. He was a disk jockey who worked further along the Peninsula.

3. Sunday had sent them all into silence and paralysis, all but an occasional real estate office or truck stop.

4. The Scope proved to be a haunt for electronics assembly people from Yoyodyne.

5. Metzger had been one of those child movie stars.

6. A clerk popped up from behind the desk where he'd been sleeping and began making sign language at her.

7. They rode over the bridge and into the great, empty glare of the Oakland afternoon.

8. She copied the diagram in her memo book.

9. Somewhere near Fillmore she found the symbol tacked to the bulletin board of a laundromat, among other scraps of paper offering cheap ironing and baby sitters.

10. The swivel chairs squeaked.

Exercise 1.5 (a) Nouns Without Determiners

The following sentences from *Breathing Lessons* by Anne Tyler contain one or more nouns or noun phrases that occur without determiners. Find them and underline them (excluding pronouns). Then give a reason why the noun or noun phrase occurs without a determiner (for example, proper noun, mass noun, abstract noun, indefinite plural noun).

1. She's always had Maggie to help her.

2. Trees were left standing, and the sidewalks ended after three blocks.

3. She would die of terror.

4. Time was running out for her.

5. She faced him, hands on her hips.

6. Fiona had started attending childbirth classes and wanted Maggie to go with her to the labor room.

7. The air smelled of rubber tires and grass.

8. Ira thudded among things in the trunk and whistled a cheerful tune.

9. She thought she could smell the coated paper that was used for Bible-study leaflets.

10. Maggie turned, but all she saw was a silhouette against a blur of yellow light.

Exercise 1.5 (b) Nouns Without Determiners

The following sentences from *Song of Solomon* by Toni Morrison contain one or more nouns or noun phrases that occur without determiners. Find them and underline them (excluding pronouns). Then give a reason why the noun or noun phrase occurs without a determiner (for example, proper noun, mass noun, abstract noun, indefinite plural noun).

1. For years he hadn't had that kind of time, or interest.

2. Life improved for Milkman enormously after he began working for Macon.

3. Amid the jokes, however, was a streak of unspoken terror.

4. Railroad Tommy laughed softly from the doorway.

5. Now all she needed was make-up.

6. She found a piece of wire, but couldn't get it through.

7. They looked into the cave and saw nothing but a great maw of darkness.

8. Milkman began to shake with hunger.

9. On autumn nights, in some parts of the city, the wind from the lake brings a sweetish smell to shore.

10. The half-dozen men there playing pool turned around at the sound of Feather's voice.

Exercise 1.5 (c) Nouns Without Determiners

The following sentences from *The Crying of Lot 49* by Thomas Pynchon contain one or more nouns or noun phrases that occur without determiners. Find them and underline them (excluding pronouns). Then give a reason why the noun or noun phrase occurs without a determiner (for example, proper noun, mass noun, abstract noun, indefinite plural noun).

1. As things developed, she was to have all manner of revelations.

2. She thought of Mucho, her husband, trying to believe in his job.

3. On the screen New Zealanders and Turks were impaling one another on bayonets.

4. It plays, as Metzger remarked later, like a Road Runner cartoon in blank verse.

5. Either way, they'll call it paranoia.

6. Heads came up at the sound of her heels, engineers stared until she'd passed, but nobody spoke to her.

7. The phone buzzed on and on, into hollowness.

8. High-pitched, comic voices issued from the TV set.

9. She began to wander aisles among light blue desks, turning a corner now and then.

10. A girl removing fake blood from her face motioned Oedipa on into a region of brightly-lit mirrors.

Exercise 1.6 (a) Pronouns

Underline the pronoun or pronouns in each of the following sentences from Wu Ch'eng-en's novel *Monkey*. Then in the space below each sentence give the person, number, and form of each pronoun (subject, object, or possessive). If the pronoun is third-person singular, give the gender as well.

1. We could really be very comfortable there.

2. As soon as dusk came, like the others, he went to his sleeping place.

3. The guardian deities rushed out and could hardly believe their eyes.

4. The brothers came to meet Erh-lang and surrounded Monkey, pressing about him on every side.

5. That was his name in religion.

6. "I don't know where the Great Sage got this trick of inviolability," said Mahabali to the Jade Emperor.

7. Neither of them had passed any of the official examinations; they were what is known as lettered countrymen.

8. "Give me back my life!" the head cried.

9. "The storm is all right," said Monkey, "provided that it happens when I want it."

10. But even should you escape this, in another five hundred years, a wind will come and blow upon you.

Exercise 1.6 (b) Pronouns

Underline the pronoun or pronouns in each of the following sentences from Basho's *The Narrow Road to the Deep North and Other Travel Sketches*. Then in the space below each sentence give the person, number, and form of each pronoun (subject, object, or possessive). If the pronoun is third-person singular, give the gender as well.

1. I left the following poem at the time of my departure from his house.

2. He changed his name to Mangiku-maru, which I liked exceedingly for its boyish flavor.

3. Let us drink under the bright beams of the moon.

4. I could not help feeling vague misgivings about the future of my journey.

5. My head is clean shaven.

6. He walked in front of me.

7. These mistakes, however, provoked frequent laughter and gave us the courage to push on.

8. The famed spring was just as it had been when the poet described it, shedding its clear drops of water with a drip-drop sound.

9. We passed through many a dangerous place, the road always winding and climbing, so that we often felt as if we were groping our way in the clouds.

10. I saw before me the aged grandmother of the young emperor taking him in her arms.

Exercise 1.6 (c) Pronouns

Underline the pronoun or pronouns in each of the following sentences from E. M. Forster's novel *A Room with a View*. Then in the space below each sentence give the person, number, and form of each pronoun (subject, object, or possessive). If the pronoun is third-person singular, give the gender as well.

1. They were tired, and under the guise of unselfishness they wrangled.

2. She knew that the intruder was ill-bred, even before she glanced at him.

3. Her face reddened with displeasure.

4. Advancing towards it very slowly and from immense distances, they touched the stone with their fingers, with their handkerchiefs, with their heads, and then retreated.

5. Her own name was Eleanor.

6. "Pardon me," said a frigid voice.

7. A very wet afternoon at the Bertolini permitted her to do the thing she really liked, and after lunch she opened the little draped piano.

8. As he touched her, his gold pince-nez became dislodged and was flattened between them.

9. On the morrow the pool had shrunk to its old size and lost its glory.

10. He was absolutely intolerable, and the same evening she broke off her engagement.

Exercise 1.7(a) Pronouns

Underline all the pronouns in the following passages from *A Room with a View*. State whether the pronoun is personal, possessive, demonstrative, or indefinite.

1. Miss Lavish spoke to it dramatically.

2. She took refuge in her dignity.

3. There are days when one sees clearly, and this is one of them.

4. Don't open the window; and you'd better draw the curtain, too; Freddy or anyone might be outside.

5. She stopped when he entered.

6. That doesn't count. I told you not Saturn.

7. He would like to throw us out, and most certainly he is justified.

8. Finally nothing happened; but the coolness remained, and for Lucy, was even increased.

9. Secrecy has this disadvantage: we lose the sense of proportion; we cannot tell whether our secret is important or not.

10. One was tired of everything, it seemed.

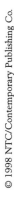

Exercise 1.7(b) Pronouns

Underline all the pronouns in the following passages from *The Narrow Road to the Deep North and Other Travel Sketches*. State whether the pronoun is personal, possessive, demonstrative, or indefinite.

1. This was the site of the warrior's house.

2. He is well known for the masculine sharpness of his wit and his habit of drinking.

3. None of these villages, however, seemed to have a distinctive local trade.

4. When dusk came, we sought a night's lodging in a humble house.

5. I attended the memorial service held for him by his brother.

6. My friends stood in a line and waved good-bye as long as they could see my back.

7. It was a cloudy day, however, and nothing but the gray sky was reflected in the pond.

8. I threw away quite a number of things, for I believed in traveling light.

9. This is probably why, even today after a thousand years, the waves break on this beach with such a melancholy sound.

10. The last two lines, in particular, impress us deeply, for they express his determination to persist in his purpose.

Exercise 1.7(c) Pronouns

Underline all the pronouns in the following passages from *Monkey*. State whether the pronoun is personal, possessive, demonstrative, or indefinite.

1. Meanwhile in Heaven everyone was wondering why a whole day had passed without any news from Erh-lang.

2. The banquet was nearing its end when one of the heavenly detectives arrived saying "The Great Sage is sticking out his head!"

3. "That is the Mountain of the Five Elements," said Hui-yen.

4. When his mother heard of it she thoroughly approved.

5. The dragons at once retired to their respective oceans.

6. "Let us rest here for a day or two before going on."

7. But Liu threw his arms about her and stopped her, saying, "Come with me, and everything will be all right."

8. He examined the incense-smoke, and was looking at the votive paintings round the walls, when someone came and announced "Another Erh-lang has arrived."

9. All of them were on the alert night and day.

10. No one could stop him, and he would have broken up the Hall of Magic Mists had not the divinity Wang Ling-Kuan rushed forward with his great metal lash.

Recognizing Verbs and Verb Phrases

Exercise 2.1(a) Verb Tense

The following sentences come from *That's Not What I Meant* by Deborah Tannen. Underline each of the verbs you find, and in the space below each sentence, write whether the verb is present tense or past tense.

1. A woman glances at a cosmetics counter.

2. Sylvia and Harry celebrated their fiftieth wedding anniversary at a mountain resort.

3. Louise ignores Jake's message.

4. As often as not, the intimate ally becomes an intimate critic.

5. He feels interrogated.

6. A similar case occurred with another pair of sisters, Lynn and Alexandra.

7. I moved on to the subject of my article.

8. Plenty of situations and individuals warrant this.

9. My research, and that of others, shows this to be untrue.

10. These incongruent expectations capture one of the key differences between men and women.

Exercise 2.1(b) Verb Tense

The following sentences come from *The Artist's Way* by Julia Cameron. Underline each of the verbs you find, and in the space below each sentence, write whether the verb is present tense or past tense.

1.   The pages emerged as a blueprint for do-it-yourself recovery.

2.   Our lives feel somehow flat.

3.   Scientists speak of it in terms of brain hemispheres.

4.   They just sounded silly.

5.   Tearfully, Cara acquiesced.

6.   No emotions scratched the surface of this man's calm.

7.   Our Censor scans our creative meadow for any dangerous beasties.

8.   Images trigger the artist brain.

9.   He located him with great embarrassment.

10.   The results of his work with them convinced him.

Exercise 2.1(c) Verb Tense

The following sentences come from *Young Men and Fire* by Norman Maclean. Underline each of the verbs you find, and in the space below each sentence, write whether the verb is present tense or past tense.

1. The men died in dead grass on the north slope.

2. Prediction by its nature depends largely upon the scientific method.

3. The tragedy offers itself as a model.

4. They reacted in seconds or less.

5. So direct testimony leaves us with opposite opinions of Hellman's closing acts.

6. A story requires movement.

7. Jansson walked up the bottom of Mann Gulch for almost half a mile.

8. This statement takes into account the Egyptian bas-relief, the drunks, and the sobbing radios.

9. The world compressed to a slit in the rocks.

10. They assembled all the relevant facts.

Exercise 2.2 (a) Verb Tense

Find and underline the past-tense verb or verbs in each of the following sentences from *That's Not What I Meant*. Then in the space below each sentence give the infinitive form of the verbs you find.

1. Murray never raised his voice nor showed emotion in it.

2. But Sharon's response felt to her like a game of one-upmanship.

3. This made Myrna angry all over again.

4. A Greek woman explained how she and her father communicated.

5. The article on summit conferences appeared in *Newsweek*, May 30, 1983.

6. In the case of the Greek father and daughter, the system worked.

7. They misread each other's frames; each stayed within his own frame.

8. Sylvia asked the advice of the others at her table.

9. The future became a present full of misunderstandings.

10. His tone of voice and facial expression gave her clues as to how he felt.

Exercise 2.2 (b) Verb Tense

Find and underline the past-tense verb or verbs in each of the following sentences from *The Artist's Way*. Then in the space below each sentence give the infinitive form of the verbs you find.

1. So you drew your first sketch?

2. He overcontrolled their best endeavors.

3. When my first marriage blew apart, I took a lonely house in the Hollywood Hills.

4. Two curves up the road behind my house, I met a gray striped cat.

5. Lewis and Clark headed west.

6. This cat lived in a vivid blue house.

7. Later that night, the moon floated above the garden.

8. I learned this quite by accident.

9. Sonia experienced doubt, fear and deepening faith.

10. The production lurched off schedule and over budget.

Exercise 2.2(c) Verb Tense

Find and underline the past-tense verb or verbs in each of the following sentences from *Young Men and Fire*. Then in the space below each sentence give the infinitive form of the verbs you find.

1. Then Dodge saw it.

2. Daylight came a little after four o'clock.

3. Ranger Jansson made the same observation.

4. When the fire struck their bodies, it blew their watches away.

5. They crossed from one geography into another.

6. They seemed big men for ghosts.

7. Dodge and Harrison rejoined the crew.

8. The deer ran straight into the first log ahead.

9. She washed me in cold water again and again.

10. A figure retreated and ascended into the sky until he hung like a bat on the roof of a cave.

Exercise 2.3(a) Auxiliary Verbs

Circle the auxiliary verbs in each of the following sentences from Maxine Hong Kingston's *The Woman Warrior*. Then underline the entire verb phrase that it introduces.

1. Not all defects could be explained so congenially.

2. I don't know any women like that, or men either.

3. I had walked into a dead land.

4. Free from families, my mother would live for two years without servitude.

5. They were eating the biggest meal of the year.

6. I was walking home.

7. I could smell the rubbery odor through the candy.

8. The Gypsy Ghosts would lure them inside.

9. The tentative first stones were falling around the crazy lady.

10. Perhaps he had looked without protection at the sky, and it had filled him.

Exercise 2.3(b) Auxiliary Verbs

Circle the auxiliary verbs in each of the following sentences from Mario Puzo's novel *The Godfather*. Then underline the entire verb phrase that it introduces.

1. His first wife was waiting for him at the door.

2. A negotiator is arranging the details.

3. He would settle this thing once and for all.

4. Everything will be OK.

5. You should know that by now.

6. They were smoothing their hair.

7. The stairs had posed a problem.

8. The Turk had become cagey.

9. His own grief would sharpen the grief of the don.

10. She was getting pleasure out of how happy he looked.

Exercise 2.3(c) Auxiliary Verbs

Circle the auxiliary verbs in each of the following sentences from Chaim Potok's novel *Davita's Harp*. Then underline the entire verb phrase that it introduces.

1. Now you will go with Baba Yaga.

2. Mrs. Helfman was talking to me.

3. I will take a little walk along the beach.

4. I think you should get yourself ready for school.

5. Aunt Sarah does not like tears.

6. The weather had turned very warm.

7. I was standing in an aisle.

8. Mama is thinking something.

9. People were shaking Mr. Dinn's hand.

10. I didn't understand how one word could have so many meanings.

Exercise 2.4 (a) Tense and Aspect

Underline the verbs or verb phrases in each of the following passages from *The Woman Warrior*. In the space below each of the passages, identify the verbs or verb phrases as: present tense; past tense; present tense with progressive aspect; or past tense with progressive aspect.

1. She works at the office.

2. One boy appeared perfect, so round in the cool opal dawn.

3. She was shivering in the corner of the seat.

4. Moon Orchid rubbed her forehead.

5. They come with trucks on Sundays.

6. Moon Orchid's daughter was helping her aunt.

7. You cool your face in tomato juice.

8. A spider headache spreads out in fine branches over my skull.

9. They smelled of milk.

10. They were joking about her.

Exercise 2.4 (b) Tense and Aspect

Underline the verbs or verb phrases in each of the following passages from *The Godfather.* In the space below each of the passages, identify the verbs or verb phrases as: present tense; past tense; present tense with progressive aspect; or past tense with progressive aspect.

1. The fear was subsiding now.

2. I am taking communion this morning.

3. Mr. Colombo nodded toward his wife.

4. His first wife was waiting for him at the door.

5. Clemenza grunted in a satisfied way.

6. It is getting bigger all the time.

7. Michael squinted down at him.

8. They were cutting the rug to fit the living room of Vito Corleone's apartment.

9. All four heads turned and stared at him.

10. Hagen dreaded the next hour.

Exercise 2.4(c) Tense and Aspect

Underline the verbs or verb phrases in each of the following passages from *Davita's Harp*. In the space below each of the passages, identify the verbs or verb phrases as: present tense; past tense; present tense with progressive aspect; or past tense with progressive aspect.

1. Jakob Daw took the glass from my mother.

2. The boys in the group were staring at me.

3. Abruptly everyone stood.

4. People were shaking Mr. Dinn's hand.

5. The weather was turning warm.

6. A long black car went slowly by.

7. I despise both communism and fascism.

8. Aunt Sarah moved about the apartment in her house slippers.

9. You are coming home from school?

10. "He looks awful," my father was saying to my mother.

Exercise 2.5 (a) Tense and Aspect

Underline the verbs or verb phrases in each of the following passages from *The Woman Warrior.* In the space below each of the passages, identify the verbs or verb phrases as present tense or past tense. In addition, if aspect is indicated in the verb phrase, write whether the aspect is progressive, perfect, or perfect progressive. Some sentences have more than one verb or verb phrase.

1. I had walked into a dead land.

2. This chair hurts me.

3. He and the other children were lying to her.

4. The plane has landed early.

5. A Chinese-American was playing Chopin.

6. The woman wore a navy blue suit with a bunch of dark cherries at the shoulder.

7. Aiaa, I am getting so old.

8. She used her sleeve.

9. Some villagers hadn't seen an airplane before.

10. Perhaps he had looked without protection at the sky, and it had filled him.

Exercise 2.5 (b) Tense and Aspect

Underline the verbs or verb phrases in each of the following passages from *The Godfather*. In the space below each of the passages, identify the verbs or verb phrases as present tense or past tense. In addition, if aspect is indicated in the verb phrase, write whether the aspect is progressive, perfect, or perfect progressive. Some sentences have more than one verb or verb phrase.

1. He was sipping from a huge glass of rye.

2. She made him coffee and served him homemade cookies in the living room.

3. Then you haven't changed much.

4. I guarantee the goods.

5. In the library the three men had relaxed.

6. The orchestra swung into the opening song of the medley.

7. He had been expecting something outrageous.

8. Clemenza spoke up in his fat man's wheeze.

9. Johnny was talking to him soothingly.

10. He had traveled with the band.

Exercise 2.5 (c) Tense and Aspect

Underline the verbs or verb phrases in each of the following passages from *Davita's Harp*. In the space below each of the passages, identify the verbs or verb phrases as present tense or past tense. In addition, if aspect is indicated in the verb phrase, write whether the aspect is progressive, perfect, or perfect progressive. Some sentences have more than one verb or verb phrase.

1.   More than one hundred people had died of the heat.

2.   I wish you strength.

3.   "You are putting the knives on the wrong side of the plate, Llana," my mother said.

4.   He seemed the most fragile person I had known.

5.   You are interrupting me!

6.   Wax was running down the candle onto David's fingers.

7.   My mother and I had come to this park with my father.

8.   It lasted about half an hour.

9.   The French appreciate my writing.

10. My mother had been sitting quietly.

Exercise 2.6 (a) Modals

Each of the passages below from *The Joy Luck Club* by Amy Tan has one or more verb phrases introduced by a modal auxiliary. Underline all the verb phrases that begin with a modal.

1. We can have stock market luck.

2. Parents should encourage instead.

3. Auntie An-mei must have bought them on Clement Street.

4. I couldn't tell by her answer if the games were different or just her attitude toward Chinese and Jewish people.

5. You will see when you are older.

6. They see daughters who will bear grandchildren.

7. I would walk by my father with a know-nothing look.

8. I could see that some terrible danger lay ahead.

9. I will remember everything about her.

10. They must wonder now how someone like me can take my mother's place.

© 1998 NTC/Contemporary Publishing Co.

Exercise 2.6 (b) Modals

Each of the passages below from *What's Eating Gilbert Grape* by Peter Hedges has one or more verb phrases introduced by a modal auxiliary. Underline all the verb phrases that begin with a modal.

1. If this keeps up, he will be too big for me to pick up.

2. I'm almost dead. Surely she can see this.

3. You might think about momma.

4. The kid would make a killing.

5. We might talk about hanging out.

6. An appointment would be most opportune.

7. That woman could have been a movie star.

8. You won't find electric doors and conveyor belts and computerized cash registers at Lamson Grocery.

9. Before she can pull it out of the way, I accelerate fast and drive over it.

10. Amy will make whatever Momma wants, and it will taste great, and Momma will clean her plate like a big girl.

Exercise 2.6 (c) Modals

Each of the passages below from *Anna Karenina* by Leo Tolstoy has one or more verb phrases introduced by a modal auxiliary. Underline all the verb phrases that begin with a modal.

1. It was settled they should go abroad.

2. He could say it without self-flattery.

3. One may give an insult.

4. She might ask for you.

5. Dolly would have soothed her, but it was too late.

6. This government clerk will go on with the thing.

7. I must tell you about that.

8. I can't tell you.

9. She understood perfectly what hope he might have.

10. The first onslaught of jealousy couldn't come back again.

Exercise 2.7(a) Tense and Aspect

Underline the verbs or verb phrases in the following sentences from *The Joy Luck Club*. In the space below each sentence, give the tense and aspect (if aspect is given in the verb phrase). Be careful; some sentences have more than one verb/verb phrase.

1. I was not those babies.

2. It would have been enough.

3. I didn't fall in the water.

4. This was her fate.

5. I must have waved my knife too close to her nose.

6. Nobody was listening to him.

7. My mother had a habit of nosiness.

8. You could become rich.

9. "Chinese people do many things," she said simply.

10. "Don't pay any attention to them," said the woman.

Exercise 2.7(b) Tense and Aspect

Underline the verbs or verb phrases in the following sentences from *Anna Karenina*. In the space below each sentence, give the tense and aspect (if aspect is given in the verb phrase). Be careful; some sentences have more than one verb/verb phrase.

1. This time Seryozha was not at home, and she was completely alone.

2. I don't know him, I don't think of him. He doesn't exist.

3. I was thinking the very same thing.

4. She would have gone, but he held her back.

5. His first steps in the world and in the service had been successful.

6. He won't understand all the gravity of this fact to us.

7. Alexey Alexandrovitch didn't attach any special significance to this tone of hers.

8. He was a general and was expecting a command.

9. She had still three hours to wait, and the memories of their last meeting set her blood in flame.

10. He would have run to her.

Exercise 2.7(c) Tense and Aspect

Underline the verbs or verb phrases in the following sentences from *What's Eating Gilbert Grape*. In the space below each sentence, give the tense and aspect (if aspect is given in the verb phrase). Be careful; some sentences have more than one verb/verb phrase.

1. Momma must have flushed.

2. This could be the happiest day of my life.

3. Beverly never writes down her orders; she has this incredible memory.

4. They do all the major burials in these parts.

5. I can't take much talk like this.

6. I don't nod.

7. Ellen is rubbing lotion on her stomach as I shift my truck into reverse.

8. She is filling my plate with coleslaw and potato salad.

9. The girl has vanished and part of me couldn't be happier.

10. As Americans we have a duty to die.

Exercise 2.8 (a) Tense and Aspect

Underline the entire verb/verb phrase in each of the following sentences from *The Joy Luck Club*. In the space below each sentence, write the tense and aspect. (Aspect is not necessarily indicated in every verb.) Some sentences may contain more than one verb/verb phrase.

1.   You will fall to the ground with the first strong wind.

2.   But these days, I think about my life's importance.

3.   She hadn't considered that Waverly might not think the same way.

4.   I cannot finish.

5.   He had left me for an opera singer.

6.   I was smiling so hard my lower lip was twitching from the strain.

7.   I dragged the metal shopping cart behind.

8.   I could see this little boy in my womb.

9.   The pendant was not a piece of jewelry I would have chosen for myself.

10. I saw what I had been fighting for.

Exercise 2.8 (b) Tense and Aspect

Underline the entire verb/verb phrase in each of the following sentences from *Anna Karenina*. In the space below each sentence, write the tense and aspect. (Aspect is not necessarily indicated in every verb.) Some sentences may contain more than one verb/verb phrase.

1. His face was dreadful from exhaustion and dismay.

2. I am losing my head all alone.

3. He has every right, and I have none.

4. She did not hear him.

5. I did not sympathize with this sudden passion.

6. The Levins had been three months in Moscow.

7. I couldn't have been so natural in your presence.

8. I'm coming directly.

9. He did not care for cards; he did not go to the club.

10. Levin, with his elbows on the balustrade, looked and listened.

Exercise 2.8(c) Tense and Aspect

Underline the entire verb/verb phrase in each of the following sentences from *What's Eating Gilbert Grape*. In the space below each sentence, write the tense and aspect. (Aspect is not necessarily indicated in every verb.) Some sentences may contain more than one verb/verb phrase.

1. I have these sudden pangs of fear.

2. Please don't mention that to my mother.

3. Mom. Mom! Uncle Dan is doing magic.

4. I can hear pro wrestling.

5. Buck Staples is working today.

6. All morning and afternoon we've been cleaning the downstairs in preparation.

7. This all might be too deep for me.

8. I've lost track of her.

9. My face doesn't even move.

10. I'm walking down the side of Highway 13, when Chip Miles pulls over in his jeep.

CHAPTER THREE

The Basic Sentence

Exercise 3.1(a) The Subject

The following sentences are taken from Alan Paton's *Cry, the Beloved Country*. Construct a yes/no question for each sentence and insert your question in the space below it; find the auxiliary and main verb in the question; and then underline the subject in your question and the corresponding word or phrase in the *original* sentence.

1. The small child opened the door.

2. Kumalo looked at his letter.

3. It had been in many hands.

4. His voice rose into loud and angry words.

5. The bus swayed from side to side.

6. The day was warm.

7. The journey had begun.

8. The door shut after him.

9. The engine is steaming again.

10. The small toy train climbs up on its narrow gauge from the valley into the hills.

Exercise 3.1 (b) The Subject

The following sentences are taken from Chaim Potok's *The Chosen*. Construct a yes/no question for each sentence and insert your question in the space below it; find the auxiliary and main verb in the question; and then underline the subject in your question and the corresponding word or phrase in the *original* sentence.

1. The five minutes were over.

2. We had lost the choosing.

3. Another short, thin boy took his place at the plate.

4. Sidney Goldberg helped me get to my feet.

5. He looked at me for a moment.

6. The teams began to disperse.

7. Danny Saunders was standing on my base.

8. My father came in a few minutes later.

9. His white shirt was pasted to his arms and back with sweat.

10. The next batter hit a long fly ball to right field.

Exercise 3.1(c) The Subject

The following sentences are taken from Bill Cosby's *Love and Marriage*. Construct a yes/no question for each sentence and insert your question in the space below it; find the auxiliary and main verb in the question; and then underline the subject in your question and the corresponding word or phrase in the *original* sentence.

1. The joke flew right by me.

2. It looks like a documentary about stags in heat.

3. All those moves were attempts to win girls.

4. I was grooming them with a toothbrush.

5. Charlene saw me with Artemis.

6. The cowboy kissed his horse.

7. A kiss was the ultimate thrill.

8. It is also an occasion of great joy.

9. Cosby discusses at length the effect of his children on his marriage.

10. The time came for me to inherit her.

Exercise 3.2(a) Adverbial Prepositional Phrases

Underline the prepositional phrase in each of the following sentences from *Love and Marriage*.

1. I was grooming them with a toothbrush.

2. This romantic agony was enriched by a less romantic one.

3. Young men no longer stand at drugstores.

4. I knew it was leading to a payoff.

5. I'm also falling in love.

6. Ruth left me for a real dancer.

7. She didn't throw a brick at me.

8. I had lost my head in beauty.

9. Charlene and I had been meant for each other.

10. I had sometimes slept with my brother.

Exercise 3.2(b) Adverbial Prepositional Phrases

Underline the prepositional phrase in each of the following sentences from *The Chosen*.

1. The head strap rubbed against the bump.

2. Mrs. Carpenter came up the aisle.

3. He looked down at me.

4. He threw the ball to Mr. Salvo.

5. He looked slowly away from the window.

6. He lay back on his pillow and closed his left eye.

7. Mr. Galanter turned to me.

8. I read in the library.

9. I stared at the prayer book.

10. His blue eyes looked dreamy for a moment.

Exercise 3.2(c) Adverbial Prepositional Phrases

Underline the prepositional phrase in each of the following sentences from *Cry, the Beloved Country.*

1. He was not speaking to them.

2. He paused for a moment.

3. Her children hid behind her skirts.

4. She reached for the Book.

5. Kumalo ate his midday meal at the Mission.

6. All roads lead to Johannesburg.

7. I do not like the way he looks at my daughter.

8. He would have played with the small boy.

9. Kumalo put his hand on his friend's arm.

10. They lie so close you cannot step over them.

Exercise 3.3(a) Adverbial Noun Phrases

Underline each adverbial noun phrase in the sentences below, taken from *Love and Marriage*.

1. Moments later, Mookie Wilson hit a meaningful grounder to deep short.

2. One afternoon I was sitting and jiggling, trying to move a coffee table farther from the door.

3. And so, one afternoon, we turned our two girls and our boy over to my mother.

4. A half hour later, you receive the right instructions.

5. A few weeks ago, I happened to say to a member of this Born Yesterday crowd, "I'm glad Miles Davis is feeling well."

6. One day she suddenly said, "Please stop doing that."

7. A few minutes later, I walked into the living room.

8. Three nights later, I walked into the Showboat with Denise.

9. A moment later, I threw myself into the broad jump.

10. One evening, I was sitting in my living room and watching the playoffs.

Exercise 3.3 (b) Adverbial Noun Phrases

Underline each adverbial noun phrase in the sentences below, taken from *The Chosen*.

1. He had been examined by a big doctor that morning.

2. One day I will tell you the reason.

3. The final exams began that Monday afternoon.

4. I dream all the time.

5. A few days later, Danny told me that his father had asked again.

6. I met Danny again in the library that week.

7. We're being moved out today.

8. Danny told me a few days later that his sister was pregnant.

9. I had this time been able to retain hold of the chain of the argument.

10. It seemed impossible to me the ball game had taken place only a week ago.

© 1998 NTC/Contemporary Publishing Co.

Exercise 3.3(c) Adverbial Noun Phrases

Underline each adverbial noun phrase in the sentences below, taken from *Cry, the Beloved Country*.

1. There's going to be a big meeting in Parkwold tomorrow night.

2. The next morning Harrison waited for his guest at the foot of the stairs.

3. Yesterday it was quite unknown.

4. That evening you will be in Ndotsheni.

5. Let us go tonight and carry them away.

6. I could have wished that he was here tonight.

7. He returned yesterday.

8. Two weeks from today, that is the day of the moving.

9. Jarvis sat a long time smoking.

10. Today it is one of the famous places of the world.

Exercise 3.4 (a) The Direct Object

The following sentences were taken from *Waiting to Exhale* by Terry McMillan. Underline the verb or verb phrase (be sure to include auxiliaries and particles in your underlining, if they occur) and bracket the direct object.

1. They didn't say a word.

2. I ordered a white Zinfandel.

3. He was wearing a cowboy tie.

4. She pushed the chair away from the table.

5. He got my deepest attention.

6. I already liked his style.

7. She couldn't even move her fingers.

8. I accepted his invitation.

9. He'd chosen the safest route.

10. He was combing Sandra's hair.

Exercise 3.4 (b) The Direct Object

The following sentences were taken from *Crazy Salad* by Nora Ephron. Underline the verb or verb phrase (be sure to include auxiliaries and particles in your underlining, if they occur) and bracket the direct object.

1. Each class carries a felt banner.

2. Almost all of us had careers.

3. I find her in the lobby.

4. Germaine Greer takes notes quietly.

5. He signs the credit agreement.

6. I am not criticizing Friedan.

7. I wanted satisfaction.

8. In the end he owns the house.

9. I love the game.

10. She now wears simple T-shirts.

Exercise 3.4 (c) The Direct Object

The following sentences were taken from *Roots* by Alex Haley. Underline the verb or verb phrase (be sure to include auxiliaries and particles in your underlining, if they occur) and bracket the direct object.

1. The older boys were opening the pens.

2. Kunta piled his wood into a bundle.

3. Then Kunta tied a slender vine about the wood.

4. Now and then, a farmer would fling his hoe.

5. He could smell the rich fragrance.

6. No men helped their wives.

7. No one could hear his mistakes.

8. Kunta knew him.

9. Others carved figures.

10. Piles of harvest dotted the fields.

Exercise 3.5 (a) Direct and Indirect Objects

Underline the transitive verb or verb phrase in each of the following sentences from *Waiting to Exhale*. Then put parentheses around each indirect object and brackets around each direct object. (Not all the sentences have an indirect object.) In the space below each sentence in which you have found an indirect object, write the test sentence you used to show that the sentence has an indirect object.

1. All three women gave me a suspicious once-over.

2. Bernadine lifted the hood.

3. I got her a two-bedroom apartment.

4. Bernadine had just told Geneva everything.

5. She clutched her purse.

6. I never trusted him in the first place.

7. Savannah lit another cigarette.

8. Bernadine stopped the car.

9. I handed him a twenty.

10. Michael lent me twenty-two hundred dollars.

Exercise 3.5 (b) Direct and Indirect Objects

Underline the transitive verb or verb phrase in each of the following sentences from *Crazy Salad*. Then put parentheses around each indirect object and brackets around each direct object. (Not all the sentences have an indirect object.) In the space below each sentence in which you have found an indirect object, write the test sentence you used to show that the sentence has an indirect object.

1. He made me an offer.

2. The League promptly appealed the decision.

3. They give women pride.

4. I loved consciousness-raising.

5. Mrs. Meir has never shown any active interest in women's rights.

6. Mandel's press secretary read her the statement.

7. These women were playing definite roles.

8. They will tell you the truth.

9. Leonard Lavin deserves a medal.

10. We had read the movement literature.

Exercise 3.5 (c) Direct and Indirect Objects

Underline the transitive verb or verb phrase in each of the following sentences from *Roots*. Then put parentheses around each indirect object and brackets around each direct object. (Not all the sentences have an indirect object.) In the space below each sentence in which you have found an indirect object, write the test sentence you used to show that the sentence has an indirect object.

1. Omoro silently handed his son a small new slingshot.

2. He caught glances of a lone rider on a horse.

3. It earned him a kick.

4. She pinched her nose.

5. He had known that hated face at first glance.

6. Bell shook her head.

7. They taught these creatures discipline.

8. A great storm had scattered the boats.

9. Kunta's seriousness conveyed his concern.

10. Kunta told Bell the news.

Exercise 3.6 (a) Direct Object and Complement

Underline the transitive verb or verb phrase in each of the following sentences from *Waiting to Exhale*. Then put square brackets around each direct object and curly brackets around each complement. (Not all sentences have a complement.) In the space below each sentence in which you have found a direct object followed by a complement, write the test sentence you used to show that the sentence has a complement.

1.   I made it strong.

2.   She'd gotten her wish.

3.   Mama, she called me a freak.

4.   She despised junk food.

5.   Bernadine owned only one decent hat.

6.   Bernadine had canceled her last two appointments.

7.   He was wearing a wedding band on his left hand.

8.   She'd open up her own little shop.

9.   Gloria heard a big truck outside her bedroom window.

10.   She ordained herself an artist.

Exercise 3.6 (b) Direct Object and Complement

Underline the transitive verb or verb phrase in each of the following sentences from *Crazy Salad*. Then put square brackets around each direct object and curly brackets around each complement. (Not all sentences have a complement.) In the space below each sentence in which you have found a direct object followed by a complement, write the test sentence you used to show that the sentence has a complement.

1. It would have made her happy.

2. He declined comment.

3. She alerted the press.

4. Her own lawyers pled her guilty.

5. She had a difficult time.

6. Her lawyer ultimately negotiated a six figure settlement.

7. Rose found herself excluded.

8. She never raised an objection.

9. Judge, we have a problem.

10. She carefully leaked information to selected reporters.

Exercise 3.6 (c) Direct Object and Complement

Underline the transitive verb or verb phrase in each of the following sentences from *Roots*. Then put square brackets around each direct object and curly brackets around each complement. (Not all sentences have a complement.) In the space below each sentence in which you have found a direct object followed by a complement, write the test sentence you used to show that the sentence has a complement.

1. He described Miss Malizy's condition.

2. He kept his ears strained.

3. Tom approached the railroad repair settlement.

4. He would call a white man a liar.

5. The chief toubob had applied grease to it.

6. He was watching this solemn rite.

7. Matilda had very little available free time.

8. He promptly issued his first order.

9. Tom made it clear.

10. He could sense the family's uneasiness.

Exercise 3.7(a) Direct Object, Indirect Object and Complement

Underline the transitive verb or verb phrase in each of the following sentences from *Jane Eyre* by Charlotte Bronte. Then put square brackets around each direct object, parentheses around each indirect object, and curly brackets around each complement.

1. I opened the glass door.

2. I had lately left a good home.

3. Call the painting "Blanche."

4. All held books in their hands.

5. She lifted her eyes.

6. I drew my gray mantle close about me.

7. Her memory gave her evidence.

8. Nothing sustained me.

9. The distant roll of wheels announced the coming coach.

10. In the evening, Bessie told me her most enchanting stories.

Name ———————————————————————— Date ————————————

Class Time ——————————————————————————

 # Exercise 3.7(b) Direct Object, Indirect Object and Complement

Underline the transitive verb or verb phrase in each of the following sentences from *Crime and Punishment* by Fyodor Dostoevsky. Then put square brackets around each direct object, parentheses around each indirect object, and curly brackets around each complement.

1. She paid him no further attention.

2. Raskolnikov opened his eyes with a start.

3. I gave the postman three copecks.

4. Well, give me the shirt.

5. That would create suspicion.

6. She showed everybody Dunya's letter.

7. He made himself very clear.

8. One small circumstance nonplussed him.

9. You won't pay her her money.

10. It would have irritated anybody.

Exercise 3.7(c) Direct Object, Indirect Object and Complement

Underline the transitive verb or verb phrase in each of the following sentences from *Wouldn't Take Nothing for My Journey Now* by Maya Angelou. Then put square brackets around each direct object, parentheses around each indirect object, and curly brackets around each complement.

1. Someone had believed that statement.

2. I find it impossible.

3. Two jobs allowed me an apartment.

4. Any observant person can acquire the same results.

5. The regulars suspended their usual world-weary demeanor.

6. She dumped the rocks along the path.

7. Nature will not abide a vacuum.

8. We must recreate a caring attitude.

9. You watch yourself about complaining.

10. A little tenderness could make life more bearable.

Exercise 3.8(a) Linking Verb, Complement, and Adverbials

Underline the linking verb in each of the following sentences from *Jane Eyre*. Then put curly brackets around each complement (noun or noun phrase or adjective or adjective phrase), and parentheses around any adverbial prepositional phrase that may complete the verb.

1. You are my wife.

2. The afternoon was wet.

3. A splashing tramp of horse-hoofs became audible.

4. I was not jealous.

5. It was deep dusk.

6. Pilot was with him.

7. The room and the house were silent.

8. I am content.

9. Dent and Lynn are in the stables.

10. I was quite ignorant.

Exercise 3.8 (b) *Linking Verb, Complement, and Adverbials*

Underline the linking verb in each of the following sentences from *Crime and Punishment*. Then put curly brackets around each complement (noun or noun phrase or adjective or adjective phrase), and parentheses around any adverbial prepositional phrase that may complete the verb.

1. Pulkheria Alexandrovna was furiously angry.

2. Razumikhin was in raptures.

3. Dunya seemed almost thunder-struck.

4. All that is gossip.

5. His dress was really too disgraceful.

6. They are such blockheads!

7. You are a base, malicious person.

8. Poverty is no crime.

9. It seemed almost providential.

10. Yes, Rodya, I am ashamed.

Exercise 3.8 (c) Linking Verb, Complement, and Adverbials

Underline the linking verb in each of the following sentences from *Wouldn't Take Nothing for My Journey Now*. Then put curly brackets around each complement (noun or noun phrase or adjective or adjective phrase), and parentheses around any adverbial prepositional phrase that may complete the verb.

1. Disbelief becomes my close companion.

2. I am brutally frank.

3. It is in the search itself.

4. She became the social maven.

5. He is not ready.

6. Here, in my finest hour, I was alone.

7. Living well is an art.

8. I seem at peace.

9. I was twenty-four, very erudite, very worldly.

10. The plague of racism is insidious.

Exercise 3.9(a) Introductory Adverbials

Each of the following sentences from *Jane Eyre* has at least one introductory adverb or adverbial phrase, either a prepositional phrase or an adverbial noun phrase. Put parentheses around each introductory adverb or adverbial, and then underline the sentence subject.

1. The next morning I was punctually opening the school.

2. In a low voice she read something.

3. By this time he had sat down.

4. In less than a month, my image will be effaced from her heart.

5. At that hour most were sewing.

6. Only this morning I received intelligence.

7. Amidst this hush the quarter sped.

8. In a few days I had recovered my health.

9. The next day a keen wind brought fresh falls.

10. At this period of my life, my heart swelled with thankfulness.

Exercise 3.9(b) Introductory Adverbials

Each of the following sentences from *Crime and Punishment* has at least one introductory adverb or adverbial phrase, either a prepositional phrase or an adverbial noun phrase. Put parentheses around each introductory adverb or adverbial, and then underline the sentence subject.

1. At first she found this burden too heavy.

2. In my personal belief you are quite right.

3. At this moment somebody knocked three times at the door.

4. Five minutes later he raised his head with a strange smile.

5. After a few more mouthfuls, Razumikhin stopped.

6. Among all these, Svidrigaylov suddenly made his appearance.

7. Another time he woke up before dawn and found himself lying on the ground.

8. Two minutes later Nastasya returned with the soup.

9. At times she shuddered and moved her eyes.

10. After her first impulse, the terrible idea seized her again.

Exercise 3.9(c) Introductory Adverbials

Each of the following sentences from *Wouldn't Take Nothing for My Journey Now* has at least one introductory adverb or adverbial phrase, either a prepositional phrase or an adverbial noun phrase. Put parentheses around each introductory adverb or adverbial, and then underline the sentence subject.

1. Besides makeup, Alvin wore a leopard print G-string.

2. On the getaway day I try for amnesia.

3. In his prayer he describes himself, his experience, and his expertise.

4. After a few years they stopped entertaining.

5. On her way back, she dumped the remaining rocks along the path.

6. On the morning I wake naturally.

7. With her high cheekbones, she looked more like an Indian chief than an old black woman.

8. The next morning she left her house carrying the meat pies.

9. In their public crudeness they have merely revealed their own vast senses of personal inferiority.

10. Too many times I have expected to reap good.

Exercise 3.10 (a) The Passive Voice

All of the following sentences from David Lodge's *Changing Places* have either active transitive verbs or verb phrases or passive verb phrases. Underline the verb or verb phrase in each sentence, and in the space below write *active* or *passive*. Remember that a passive voice verb phrase *must* include the *be* auxiliary *and* the past participle of the main verb.

1. The plane might be struck by a thunderbolt.

2. Morris Zapp experiences a rush of missionary zeal to the head.

3. The commentaries would not be designed for the general reader.

4. On his way back he verifies his suspicion.

5. He was prevented from entering by a ring of campus policemen.

6. He was prepared to settle for Works Foreman.

7. Invariably they caused disciplinary problems.

8. He was asked two questions at the party.

9. Philip was not allowed to forget his existence.

10. Euphoria had been settled by a narrow-minded Puritanical sect.

Exercise 3.10 (b) The Passive Voice

All of the following sentences from Bharati Mukherjee's *Jasmine* have either active transitive verbs or verb phrases or passive verb phrases. Underline the verb or verb phrase in each sentence, and in the space below write *active* or *passive*. Remember that a passive voice verb phrase *must* include the *be* auxiliary *and* the past participle of the main verb.

1. I treat him as an innocent.

2. At dinner Bud snapped Darrel's head off.

3. The farmer was known to have four sons.

4. His mind is closed against me.

5. She shrugged her thanks.

6. A busload of Hindus was hijacked.

7. Mother Ripplemeyer tells me her Depression stories.

8. I watch the patterns on the ceiling.

9. He is called Yogi in school.

10. Bud was wounded in the war between my fate and my will.

Exercise 3.10 (c) The Passive Voice

All of the following sentences from L. M. Montgomery's *Anne of Green Gables* have either active transitive verbs or verb phrases or passive verb phrases. Underline the verb or verb phrase in each sentence, and in the space below write *active* or *passive*. Remember that a passive voice verb phrase *must* include the *be* auxiliary *and* the past participle of the main verb.

1. Her dishes were washed.

2. I named that cherry tree.

3. The child was quite transfigured.

4. One of the doors was broken.

5. Anne clasped her hands.

6. Matthew opened the yard gate for them.

7. She was shocked by the scandalous thing.

8. Anne garlanded her hat with a heavy wreath.

9. She should be taught a prayer the very next day.

10. Marilla asked no more questions.

CHAPTER FOUR

Adding Details with Modifiers

Exercise 4.1(a) Prepositional Phrases

Find the prepositional phrases in the following sentences from *Changing Places*. Put parentheses around each one and then underline the entire noun phrase that includes it.

1. The end of the Gutenberg era was evidently not an issue here.

2. It contained a hand-written letter from Philip Swallow.

3. He opened the other drawers in the desk.

4. There was a flurry of activity.

5. The darkness of the room made this seem more plausible.

6. He telephoned the Chairman of the Department.

7. Philip missed the expected note of outrage and fear.

8. There was still hope for Ireland.

9. The hour for tea had arrived.

10. The sight of all this unsolicited booty made him slightly delirious.

Exercise 4.1 (b) Prepositional Phrases

Find the prepositional phrases in the following sentences from *Jasmine*. Put parentheses around each one and then underline the entire noun phrase that includes it.

1. Bhindranwale was the leader of all the fanatics.

2. A hair from some peasant's head could save an American meteorologist's reputation.

3. Sunlight smeared one wall of windows.

4. My note to the professor had been properly self-condemning.

5. She blamed impurities in the food.

6. The boys in my village caught the house lizards.

7. The rest of the night seemed unstoppable and unbearable.

8. An adjacent shop under the same ownership sold sweets and spices.

9. It was just a crude gap in the mud wall.

10. This man is a danger to us.

Exercise 4.1(c) Prepositional Phrases

Find the prepositional phrases in the following sentences from *Anne of Green Gables*. Put parentheses around each one and then underline the entire noun phrase that includes it.

1. I'll take twenty pounds of sugar.

2. Mrs. Barry was a woman of strong prejudices.

3. She bent down and kissed the flushed cheek on the pillow.

4. The rivalry between them was soon apparent.

5. An old piano scarf of yellow crepe was an excellent substitute.

6. The whole character of the room was altered.

7. The program that night was a series of "thrills."

8. She is cultivating a spirit of humility.

9. The firs in the Haunted Wood were all feathery and wonderful.

10. She and Anne exchanged furtive smiles of guilty amusement.

Exercise 4.2(a) Appositives

Put one line under each appositive in the following passages from *Changing Places*. Then put a double line under the noun or noun phrase that is modified by the appositive. In the space below, write whether the appositive is restrictive or nonrestrictive.

1. The gas attack was authorized by Miranda County Sheriff Hank O'Keene.

2. Professor Morris J. Zapp, a visiting professor, has been suggested as a possible candidate for the job of mediator.

3. The owner of the house, Dr. Brendan O'Shea, said this morning, "I'm flabbergasted."

4. Now people, complete strangers, come up to me and shake my hand.

5. It was your Irish girl, the toothless Bernadette, who betrayed you.

6. There is doubt, too, whether Governor Duck, a member of the University Council, would allow the lease to be approved.

7. Howard Ringbaum, a prime suspect, has been offered a job in Canada.

8. Rupert Sutcliffe shuffled in, a tall, stooped, melancholy figure.

9. He was a short, bespectacled man with thinning hair—a disappointingly unheroic figure.

10. Professor Gordon H. Masters, Professor of English at Rummidge University, yesterday tendered his resignation to the Vice-Chancellor.

Exercise 4.2(b) Appositives

Put one line under each appositive in the following passages from *Jasmine*. Then put a double line under the noun or noun phrase that is modified by the appositive. In the space below, write whether the appositive is restrictive or nonrestrictive.

1.   All the apartments belonged to Columbia teachers, true professors.

2.   My brothers, generous men, couldn't get together fifty thousand.

3.   Jasmine, the caregiver, was eager to lavish care on the family.

4.   Wylie and Taylor and their little girl, Duff, met us with tea and biscuits.

5.   One day he outfitted Jasmine, child of the Indian pampas, in a lavender ski suit.

6.   For every Jasmine the reliable caregiver, there is a Jase the prowling adventurer.

7.   The name Harlan Kroener wasn't red-flagged in any way.

8.   Karin, Bud's ex, once called me a gold digger.

9.   Wednesdays are Mother's days to have lunch with Mrs. Bloomquist, the potato-faced woman.

10. Orrin Lacey, the Agricultural Loans man, helped Bud change into pajamas.

Exercise 4.2(c) Appositives

Put one line under each appositive in the following passages from *Anne of Green Gables*. Then put a double line under the noun or noun phrase that is modified by the appositive. In the space below, write whether the appositive is restrictive or nonrestrictive.

1. There is a piece in the Fifth Reader—"The Downfall of Poland"—that is just full of thrills.

2. The trustees have hired a new teacher, Miss Muriel Stacy.

3. It was almost noon when they found their way to "Beechwood," a fine, old mansion.

4. Through Newbridge, a bustling little village, they drove, still in silence.

5. There was a passenger—a little girl.

6. Even Bell, the superintendent, came by.

7. You're doing a mighty foolish thing—a risky thing.

8. Thomas Lynde, a meek little man, was sowing his late turnip seed on the hill field beyond the barn.

9. All the little wood things—the ferns and the satin leaves and the crackerberries—have gone to sleep.

10. She had made friends with the spring—the wonderful, deep, clear, icy-cold spring.

Exercise 4.3 (a) Nonrestrictive Appositives and Adjective Phrases

Put a single line under each nonrestrictive appositive or adjective phrase in the following sentences from *Of Mice and Men* by John Steinbeck. Then put a double line under the noun or noun phrase that is modified.

1. At his heels there walked a dragfooted sheep dog, gray of muzzle.

2. At that moment a young man came into the bunk house, a thin young man with a brown face.

3. We're going to have a little place of our own, a house and a garden.

4. A lady, my own Aunt Clara, gave me some velvet.

5. His hands, large and lean, were as delicate in their action as those of a temple dancer.

6. Old Candy, the swamper, came in and went to his bunk.

7. He had books, too, a tattered dictionary and a mauled copy of the California civil code for 1905.

8. Take Curley, my husband. His hair is just like wire.

9. He unrolled his bundle and put things on the shelf, his razor, bar of soap, and comb.

10. Behind him walked a huge man, shapeless of face.

Exercise 4.3 (b) Nonrestrictive Appositives and Adjective Phrases

Put a single line under each nonrestrictive appositive or adjective phrase in the following sentences from *Mr. Sammler's Planet* by Saul Bellow. Then put a double line under the noun or noun phrase that is modified.

1. The doctor is a hillbilly, a Georgia red-neck.

2. Pictures could do a job on Lindsay, the mayor.

3. Arkin, a good man, was missed.

4. The world, Riverside Drive, was wickedly lighted up.

5. He had had some talks with one of his younger relations, Angela Gruner.

6. Such was Sammler's eastward view, a soft asphalt belly.

7. Underfoot was the respectable carpet, brown as gravy.

8. The manicurist, heavy-shouldered, bent with instruments over his nails.

9. Hessid, a fine-looking old man with a broad white beard, wore a derby.

10. The night table, copper-lined, kept things fresh.

Exercise 4.3 (c) Nonrestrictive Appositives and Adjective Phrases

Put a single line under each nonrestrictive appositive or adjective phrase in the following sentences from *One Hundred Years of Solitude* by Gabriel García Márquez. Then put a double line under the noun or noun phrase that is modified.

1. They were put in the care of Visita-ción, a Guajiro Indian woman.

2. Active, small, severe, Visita-ción seemed to be everywhere.

3. It was a thick night, starless.

4. The only one who accepted was Aureliano Triste, a big man with his grandfather's drive.

5. He had a blind rage, a broad feeling of impotence.

6. They were new gypsies, young men and women.

7. Serene now, they tried to separate Úrsula's gold from the debris that was stuck to the bottom of the pot.

8. Cataure, the Indian, was gone from the house by morning.

9. Several friends of José Arcadio Buendía, young men like him, dismantled their houses and packed up.

10. The discovery of the galleon, an indication of the proximity of the sea, broke his drive.

Exercise 4.4(a) Participle Phrases

Put a line under each of the participle phrases in the following sentences from *Breathing Lessons* by Anne Tyler. Then put a double line under the noun or noun phrase it modifies. In the space below each sentence, write whether the participle is restrictive or nonrestrictive.

1. Finally there came Jesse, walking doubled over between two officers.

2. She fluttered around her, looking inadequate.

3. Judging from the way those balloons were bobbing about, he guessed his cards might blow away.

4. Like a tailor measuring a half-dressed client, Ira remained discreetly sightless.

5. He did have Maggie, eventually—dropping into his lap like a wonderful gift out of nowhere.

6. Clinging to Ira's arm with both hands, Junie walked to the pharmacy.

7. Intending to be hard on his son, Ira had insisted his wife stay home.

8. The traffic signal, turning green, was the one little pinprick of color.

9. She stepped up onto the curb, gaping all the while.

10. "That's him, all right," Mr. Otis said, rising by inches from his seat.

Exercise 4.4 (b) Participle Phrases

Put a line under each of the participle phrases in the following sentences from *Mr. Sammler's Planet*. Then put a double line under the noun or noun phrase it modifies. In the space below each sentence, write whether the participle is restrictive or nonrestrictive.

1. Referring to himself, Sammler once had observed, "I am more stupid about some things than about others."

2. In Spanish Morocco he was robbed in his hotel by a man with a gun, hidden in his closet.

3. Wallace, taking a young lady to see the film *The Birth of a Child*, fainted away at the actual moment of birth.

4. I can remember Shula years ago in New Rochelle, coming downstairs in her nightgown.

5. She must have been twenty-seven or so, kneeling in front of everybody in the parlor.

6. Someone ahead, carrying the light, stumbled and faltered.

7. Wallace, borrowing his father's Rolls, let it somehow get away from him.

8. Turning from the new New York of massed apartments, Sammler saw through large black circles in a fence daffodils and tulips.

9. Tapping the flagstones every fourth step, Sammler held Dr. Lal's manuscript under his arm.

10. The moon caught the eye of Wallace, drinking in the back seat.

Exercise 4.4(c) Participle Phrases

Put a line under each of the participle phrases in the following sentences from *One Hundred Years of Solitude*. Then put a double line under the noun or noun phrase it modifies. In the space below each sentence, write whether the participle is restrictive or nonrestrictive.

1. They were, after all, schoolchildren playing at being grown-ups.

2. Whipping him without mercy, she chased him to the back of the courtyard.

3. They would sit on the porch, suffocated by the oregano and the roses.

4. "I've been to this park in Florence," Pietro Crespi would say, going through the cards.

5. Arcadio waited for her that night, trembling with fever in his hammock.

6. Poring over the manuscripts, he sensed that he was not alone in the room.

7. "It was Aureliano," she shouted, running toward the chestnut tree.

8. A few yards away, sleeping in a hammock, he was not aware of anything.

9. He spent the night awake, tormented by the pain of his sores.

10. Aureliano José, dressed as a revolutionary officer, gave him military honors.

Exercise 4.5 (a) Relative Clauses

Underline each of the relative clauses you find in the sentences below. Then put a double line under the noun or noun phrase it modifies. In the space below the sentence, write whether the relative clause is restrictive or nonrestrictive. These sentences come from *Breathing Lessons*.

1. She craned back to look at them and so did Dorrie, who was hanging on his other arm.

2. Maggie murmured encouragement to his father, whose breathing was growing louder.

3. The front door was the kind without those tiny glass panes that are placed too high to be useful.

4. The person who stands at the door makes you give your name and address.

5. Maggie felt a sense of frustration that was almost suffocating.

6. Nobody else was in sight except for a single balloon man, who took shape eerily on the opposite corner.

7. Leroy was one of those babies who fling themselves off stair landings.

8. She glanced up to see Fiona and a slightly older girl, who must have been her sister.

9. I'd have to open four cans before I had leftovers that weren't in fractions.

10. Maggie wondered if a backpack was one of the pieces of equipment Jesse considered essential.

Exercise 4.5 (b) Relative Clauses

Underline each of the relative clauses you find in the sentences below. Then put a double line under the noun or noun phrase it modifies. In the space below the sentence, write whether the relative clause is restrictive or nonrestrictive. These sentences come from *Mr. Sammler's Planet*.

1. One of them had on just the sort of little cap that Angela wore.

2. He couldn't bear to face windows which nothing but blue sky was visible through.

3. They had been quarreling with their lovers, who were now lying in the road on their bellies.

4. Sammler heard him give this protest through his teeth, which were bad and tiny.

5. He dressed in narrow gray-denim garments, obviously old stock that had been palmed off on him.

6. The embarrassment is terrible, being the father of a woman-lunatic who ambushes this unhappy Indian.

7. Tolstoy says you don't kill another human being whom you have exchanged such a look with.

8. Dr. Lal had a report from the detective who visited her today.

9. Oh, Uncle, suppose I were a zoologist who had never seen a live leviathan.

10. How could the ignorant nonspecialist confront these technical miracles which made him a sort of uncomprehending savage?

Exercise 4.5 (c) Relative Clauses

Underline each of the relative clauses you find in the sentences below. Then put a double line under the noun or noun phrase it modifies. In the space below the sentence, write whether the relative clause is restrictive or nonrestrictive. These sentences come from *One Hundred Years of Solitude*.

1.   There were many people who had sufficient insight.

2.   He assumed an attitude that was quite childish.

3.   The government made the official announcement in a high-sounding proclamation, which promised merciless punishment.

4.   Petra Cotes would be the one who would bring about the break.

5.   She left the house in a coach that had to travel only two blocks to take her to the convent.

6.   When he asked for the most beautiful woman who had ever been seen on earth, all the women brought him their daughters.

7.   She had never heard mention of the wars that were bleeding the country.

8.   In the manor house, which was paved with tomblike slabs, the sun was never seen.

9.   Fernanda was a woman who was lost in the world.

10.   All that was left was the furniture that was absolutely necessary.

Exercise 4.6 (a) Relative Clauses

Underline each of the relative clauses you find in the sentences below, including relative clauses modifying words of place or time. Then put a double line under the noun or noun phrase it modifies. In the space below the sentence, write whether the relative clause is restrictive or nonrestrictive. These sentences come from Emily Bronte's novel *Wuthering Heights*.

1. The ledge, where I placed my candle, had a few mildewed books piled up in one corner.

2. This was Zillah, the stout housewife, who at length issued forth to inquire into the nature of the uproar.

3. I landed in the back-kitchen, where a gleam of fire enabled me to rekindle my candle.

4. I'll demolish the first who puts me out of temper!

5. Nothing was stirring except a gray cat, which crept from the ashes.

6. It opened into the house, where the females were already astir.

7. Mrs. Heathcliff walked to a seat far off, where she kept her word by playing the part of a statue.

8. It lies in a hollow whose peaty moisture is said to embalm the few corpses deposited there.

9. The unfortunate lad is the only one that does not guess how he has been cheated.

10. He smothered the storm in a brutal curse, which I took care not to notice.

Exercise 4.6 (b) Relative Clauses

Underline each of the relative clauses you find in the sentences below, including relative clauses modifying words of place or time. Then put a double line under the noun or noun phrase it modifies. In the space below the sentence, write whether the relative clause is restrictive or nonrestrictive. These sentences come from Donna Tartt's novel *The Secret History*.

1. I think Bunny's about the only person in the world who can make Henry laugh.

2. This was a Friday, which meant no classes.

3. One of them hopped clumsily to the end of a branch, which squeaked and bobbed under its weight.

4. The only time of day I had been able to stand was the very early morning, when the streets were empty and the light was golden and kind on the dry grass.

5. Much of the talk centered around events which I was not privy to.

6. I suppose there is a certain crucial interval in everyone's life when character is fixed forever.

7. Except for Julian, who always made a point of arriving a few minutes late, everyone was there.

8. On the mantel of the fireplace, which I later discovered was inoperable, glittered a pair of lead-glass candelabra.

9. We went to the greyhound track in Pownal, where he ended up bringing home a dog too old to race.

10. It was the only card game that Bunny knew.

Exercise 4.6(c) Relative Clauses

Underline each of the relative clauses you find in the sentences below, including relative clauses modifying words of place or time. Then put a double line under the noun or noun phrase it modifies. In the space below the sentence, write whether the relative clause is restrictive or nonrestrictive. These sentences come from Gabriel García Márquez's novel *Love in the Time of Cholera*.

1. They also brought in an anaconda, whose insomniac hunter's sighs disturbed the darkness in the bedrooms.

2. The Doctor's final doubts collapsed one night when the thieves tried to get in again through a skylight in the attic.

3. One rainy afternoon he encountered a disaster in the house that brought him to his senses.

4. From December through March, when the nights were cold and the north winds made living outdoors unbearable, he was taken inside to sleep in the bedrooms in a cage covered by a blanket.

5. She consoled herself with color illustrations from Linnaeus's *Natural History*, which she framed and hung on the drawing room walls.

6. The bedroom was large and bright, with two windows open to the trees in the patio, where one could hear the clamor of cicadas.

7. One of the German mastiffs, maddened by a sudden attack of rabies, had torn to pieces every animal that crossed its path.

8. He evoked the nostalgia of the lighthouse in his old age when he had everything settled.

9. Fermina Daza, whose straightforward character had become more subtle with the years, seized on her husband's casual words.

10. His first sign of life was a cough that seemed intended to awaken her.

Exercise 4.7(a) Adverbial Subordinate Clauses

Underline the adverbial subordinate clause in each of the following sentences from *Wuthering Heights*. In the space below each sentence, write the general meaning relationship that holds between the subordinate and main clause (time, cause, condition, concession, or purpose).

1. The animal followed its mistress upstairs, when she went to bed.

2. "What a noise for nothing!" I cried, though rather uneasy myself.

3. Heathcliff frequently visits the Grange, though on the strength of the mistress having known him when he was a boy.

4. There was a bare possibility of overtaking them if they were pursued instantly.

5. "What ails you, Cathy?" he was saying when I entered.

6. Her teeth chattered as she shrank closer to the embers.

7. I shall never forget the scene when we reached her chamber.

8. The doctor spoke hopefully of the case having a favorable end, if we could preserve around her constant tranquillity.

9. "I have waited here an hour," he resumed, while I continued staring.

10. I've fought through a bitter life since I last heard your voice.

Exercise 4.7(b) Adverbial Subordinate Clauses

Underline the adverbial subordinate clause in each of the following sentences from *The Secret History*. In the space below each sentence, write the general meaning relationship that holds between the subordinate and main clause (time, cause, condition, concession, or purpose).

1. Though Bunny wasn't with us, he'd have a hard time proving he wasn't.

2. I had noticed its absence while I was packing.

3. Even if there was a side of him of which I was unaware, was it possible that he was attracted to her?

4. I stood there, holding the receiver, until a dial tone came droning on the other end.

5. The dining halls were open, though at that hour of the morning there were no students.

6. As I drank my coffee and gazed around the dining room, it struck me that Georges Laforgue had been right after all.

7. He came by last night while I was really sleepy.

8. When the ground rose several hours later, we came upon another, smaller party.

9. He pretended not to see us until it was impossible for him to ignore us any longer.

10. If I hurried I could be there in fifteen minutes.

Exercise 4.7(c) Adverbial Subordinate Clauses

Underline the adverbial subordinate clause in each of the following sentences from *Love in the Time of Cholera*. In the space below each sentence, write the general meaning relationship that holds between the subordinate and main clause (time, cause, condition, concession, or purpose).

1. She decided against the idea because that might be just what he wanted.

2. He experienced no emotion when he met the woman.

3. It closed its eyes when it was laid down.

4. For half an hour the two of them had to amuse themselves with the birdcages while Fermina Daza finished her bath.

5. You cannot come in now because her papa is not at home.

6. Fermina Daza was in the sewing room when he appeared at the window.

7. She arrived with crates of live turkeys and all the fruits of her fertile lands so that no one would lack for food during her visit.

8. As she spoke, she pulled from her sleeve a gold rosary with Christ carved in marble.

9. She would pass by the telegraph office on Wednesday afternoons so that he could place her lover's answers in her hand.

10. He talked too much when he was making house calls.

Exercise 4.8 (a) Adverbial Infinitive Phrases

Underline the adverbial infinitive phrases in the sentences below. Be careful not to mistake a prepositional phrase beginning with *to* for an infinitive phrase; remember that infinitive phrases have infinitive verbs following *to*, and not a noun or noun phrase. These sentences are taken from *Wuthering Heights*.

1. All I learned was on occasion of going to aid in the preparations for the funeral.

2. Mr. Kenneth came to announce the event to my master.

3. The lawyer was called to get his instructions.

4. I explained that I had come to see everything carried on decently.

5. No thought of worldly affairs crossed his mind to disturb him.

6. I remember stopping to kick the breath out of him.

7. He flew to answer this.

8. I was never hired to serve you.

9. She wrote to inform her brother of the probable conclusion.

10. I've come to fetch you home.

Exercise 4.8 (b) Adverbial Infinitive Phrases

Underline the adverbial infinitive phrases in the sentences below. Be careful not to mistake a prepositional phrase beginning with *to* for an infinitive phrase; remember that infinitive phrases have infinitive verbs following *to*, and not a noun or noun phrase. These sentences are taken from *The Secret History.*

1.   All the scientists in the world united to avert the catastrophe.

2.   I guess Camilla went over to say hello to Hugh.

3.   Searchers milled curiously in the snowy background, raising on tiptoe to jeer silently at the camera.

4.   Why had no one been by to get me?

5.   My reflection rose to meet me head-on in the opposite mirror.

6.   Did I tell you that some men came round to see me?

7.   I liked especially wandering down the river bank to drink a bottle of wine.

8.   I told Francis that the FBI men had done it to watch his eyes get round.

9.   He was really wigged out and asked if he could borrow Bram's car last night, to leave school.

10.   He sometimes left a saucer of milk outside his door to appease any malevolent spirits.

Exercise 4.8 (c) Adverbial Infinitive Phrases

Underline the adverbial infinitive phrases in the sentences below. Be careful not to mistake a prepositional phrase beginning with *to* for an infinitive phrase; remember that infinitive phrases have infinitive verbs following *to*, and not a noun or noun phrase. These sentences are taken from *Love in the Time of Cholera*.

1. At least now he could live without seeing Fermina Daza, instead of interrupting whatever he was doing to search for her.

2. They would cross the street to walk on the other side.

3. She went to meet Florentino Ariza in the telegraph office.

4. She turned her head to hear.

5. In order to avoid questions she did not wear mourning clothes.

6. She rushed to take refuge in her cabin.

7. She had done little more than leave her house to go to school.

8. Many times the yellow plague flag had been flown in order to evade taxes.

9. For a long time he had boarded ships just to drink a glass of water from the village where he was born.

10. He went back to his native country as if it were one of those little trips one takes to ward off nostalgia.

© 1998 NTC/Contemporary Publishing Co.

Exercise 4.9 (a) Avoiding Fragments

Identify the following passages as fragments or complete sentences. For each fragment, try to give a reason why it does not qualify as a sentence (for example, noun phrase, relative clause, adverbial subordinate clause). These passages are taken from *Zen and the Art of Motorcycle Maintenance* by Robert M. Pirsig.

1. Until there was nothing left to stand.

2. He had broken the code.

3. It all gave way from under him.

4. The image of nothingness.

5. Which are the continuity of quality.

6. He can be considerate when he's in the mood.

7. Very unimportant.

8. Mountain spring water has the best taste in the world.

9. Geometry is not true; it is advantageous.

10. With each additional growth.

Exercise 4.9 (b) Avoiding Fragments

Identify the following passages as fragments or complete sentences. For each fragment, try to give a reason why it does not qualify as a sentence (for example, noun phrase, relative clause, adverbial subordinate clause). These passages are also taken from *Zen and the Art of Motorcycle Maintenance*.

1.   The same is true of hypotheses.

2.   Not a coffin, a sarcophagus.

3.   We first seek the cases in which this rule has the greatest chance of failing.

4.   About the trip.

5.   Crunchy gravel on the road.

6.   A wave of crystallization had taken place.

7.   I feel grateful.

8.   To be at one with this goodness.

9.   We stretch our legs for a while.

10.   A person who lived here once.

Exercise 4.9(c) Avoiding Fragments

Identify the following passages as fragments or complete sentences. For each fragment, try to give a reason why it does not qualify as a sentence (for example, noun phrase, relative clause, adverbial subordinate clause). These passages are also taken from *Zen and the Art of Motorcycle Maintenance*.

1. A connecting-rod.

2. Sleep is gone.

3. On the road now.

4. Big trees that almost completely cover the road.

5. A wisp of fog has appeared above the creek.

6. In this desert-like country.

7. The attendant still doesn't show.

8. Until it gets worse or better.

9. That is gumption.

10. Looking at the glass door.

CHAPTER FIVE

Content Clauses and Verbals

Exercise 5.1(a) Content Clauses as Direct Objects

Each of the following sentences from *The Temple of My Familiar* by Alice Walker has a content clause that is a direct object of a verb of thinking or speaking. Underline the content clause once and put a double line under the verb or verb phrase to which it serves as direct object.

1. The men forgot that they had made them so.

2. At first she thought it was hatred.

3. She could not know that every word about Arveyda was a dagger.

4. Uncle Isaac said he searched each photograph carefully.

5. He didn't know that one of their skills was the ability to read minds.

6. She realized she had never known Zedé at peace.

7. They thought I was waving good-bye.

8. Suwelo realized with a start that in his real life he was never around old people.

9. She knew he had written it.

10. When he learned there would be a Jewish state, he accepted it as an excuse to go back.

Exercise 5.1(b) Content Clauses as Direct Objects

Each of the following sentences from *The War of the Saints* by Jorge Amado has a content clause that is a direct object of a verb of thinking or speaking. Underline the content clause once and put a double line under the verb or verb phrase to which it serves as direct object.

1. He realized that this "model" had sent the copy to Portugal.

2. He'd said he wanted to be the first.

3. You must promise me that you won't let it out.

4. I've just learned that something unforeseen has caused a small delay.

5. He knew Adalgisa was chaste.

6. He suspected that she'd been fooling around with her boyfriend.

7. He knew that in the afternoon whiskey was served.

8. She thinks she's carrying the king in her belly.

9. Dom Maximiliano von Gruden didn't believe that the devil had anything to do with it.

10. Since the image is so valuable, I can't say that he's wrong.

Exercise 5.1(c) Content Clauses as Direct Objects

Each of the following sentences from *A Red Death* by Walter Mosley has a content clause that is a direct object of a verb of thinking or speaking. Underline the content clause once and put a double line under the verb or verb phrase to which it serves as direct object.

1. I just thought you wanted to know.

2. I soon realized that there was nothing for me to consider.

3. He was probably wondering if the next landlord would use him.

4. Back then we thought we knew who the enemy was.

5. Then I remembered that she belonged to another man.

6. You know we broke up years ago.

7. She said I should come up here, away from all that.

8. I was wondering if Mouse could kill me.

9. He knew that nobody was better than him.

10. I wondered if Agent Craxton had political aspirations.

Exercise 5.2 (a) Content Clauses as Indirect Speech

Each of the following sentences from *The Temple of My Familiar* includes direct quotation. Rewrite each sentence so that a content clause replaces the quoted speech.

1. "Good writers do that," he murmured.

2. "They've printed a second edition," she said.

3. "This is my daughter from America," he said proudly.

4. "I'm leaving," said Suwelo, stretching and getting to his feet.

5. "Aren't they all the same name, more or less?" he asked.

6. "Was this a real person?" asked Kesselbaum.

7. "Many people have passionate interests in historical figures," said the shrink.

8. "I don't know," she said.

9. "I wouldn't mind dying if dying was all," Miss Lissie told Suwelo.

10. "She is about our age," Fanny wrote.

Exercise 5.2 (b) Content Clauses as Indirect Speech

Each of the following sentences from *The War of the Saints* includes direct quotation. Rewrite each sentence so that a content clause replaces the quoted speech.

1. "It's worth a fortune," he said.

2. "Miracles happen," the abbot said.

3. "I'm only a threatened priest," Father Abelardo wrote.

4. "I came to add the final touches," he said.

5. Danilo commented, "Everybody's talking about that business of the statue."

6. "The family is the backbone of society," the landowner would say.

7. "It wasn't the governor," Olímpia would answer.

8. "The taping must just be starting," he explained.

9. "I don't understand," he said.

10. "This place is crawling with cops," Nilda told Nelson.

Exercise 5.2(c) Content Clauses as Indirect Speech

Each of the following sentences from *A Red Death* includes direct quotation. Rewrite each sentence so that a content clause replaces the quoted speech.

1. "My car is the Ford out front," I said.

2. "Thirteen hundred was all they had left," I said.

3. "They set me up," he said.

4. "The envelope was the kind they used for the distribution list?" I asked.

5. "We can't just leave him here," Shirley said.

6. "Poppa slept on the couch," she added.

7. "It depends on where you come from," I said.

8. "Shirley's a good girl," Chaim said.

9. "Did some woman really die?" she asked.

10. "I talked to your friend the other day, Easy," Agent Craxton said.

Exercise 5.3 (a) Content Clauses

The following sentences from *The Temple of My Familiar* all contain content clauses. Underline each content clause you find, and in the space below the sentence, write whether the clause is a subject, an object, or a complement.

1.   Suwelo could hardly believe he was tasting this dish for the first time.

2.   I thought I loved Suwelo.

3.   She felt she didn't exist to anyone.

4.   I see that it really needs me.

5.   Some of our friends thought we had separated.

6.   She found she enjoyed living in her own mess.

7.   Zedé never conceded that there were any such people as heathens.

8.   She did not think she still loved him.

9.   Fanny thought it probably didn't fit anybody.

10.   It seemed that he was mostly talking to the crabs.

Exercise 5.3(b) Content Clauses

The following sentences from *The War of the Saints* all contain content clauses. Underline each content clause you find, and in the space below the sentence, write whether the clause is a subject, an object, or a complement.

1. From the sound of your voice, I can see that you're in torment.

2. It is often said that a person who suffers develops great forbearance.

3. I think she's sick.

4. The problem was that she could not see.

5. He hadn't known that his friend Tibúrcio would be coming with a lady.

6. They shouldn't forget that, in his view, the husband was the head of the family.

7. It was known that she was carrying his baby in her belly.

8. I hope that your guardian will reverse the decision.

9. The inspector realized that he was participating in a demonstration.

10. The professor told him he'd seen Manela.

Exercise 5.3(c) Content Clauses

The following sentences from *A Red Death* all contain content clauses. Underline each content clause you find, and in the space below the sentence, write whether the clause is a subject, an object, or a complement.

1. I knew the family would be downstairs.

2. It was a given that he was talking to me.

3. Primo thought I was less than rational.

4. Roberta said that the board was hiring.

5. I never knew if he remembered anything about the past.

6. Dad thought they'd take him.

7. That he stole the papers from Wenzler was still uncertain.

8. He once told me that the town was mobile.

9. He said that he was selling life insurance.

10. I was amazed to think that the apartments were still my property.

Exercise 5.4 (a) Verbals as Direct Objects

Each of the following sentences from Isabel Allende's novel *The House of the Spirits* contains a verbal as a direct object, either as an infinitive phrase or a participle phrase. Find the verbal, underline it, and then put a double line under the verb or verb phrase to which it serves as object. In the space below the sentence, write whether the verbal is an infinitive phrase or a participle phrase.

1. Marcos did not want to disappoint them.

2. Nana suggested cutting off his tail.

3. No political gathering managed to attract so many people.

4. He learned to manage these fits.

5. Clara continued staring at the sky.

6. He planned to take off in his bird.

7. Nana began to suffer dizzy spells from being on her feet all day.

8. People began to speculate that he had disappeared.

9. The ants continued to climb.

10. He wanted to appear taller.

Exercise 5.4(b) Verbals as Direct Objects

Each of the following sentences from Dean Koontz's novel *Sole Survivor* contains a verbal as a direct object, either as an infinitive phrase or a participle phrase. Find the verbal, underline it, and then put a double line under the verb or verb phrase to which it serves as object. In the space below the sentence, write whether the verbal is an infinitive phrase or a participle phrase.

1. She and Henry had enjoyed watching fireflies from their back porch.

2. Friends had tried to comfort him after the catastrophe.

3. Joe could not bear to watch them.

4. At the funeral, both Joe and Henry had needed to lean on Beth.

5. He wanted to feel the pain.

6. He liked to listen to her talk.

7. He considered packing and leaving.

8. He couldn't bear to voice his doubt.

9. Joe could not remember acting so bold.

10. He now wanted to live.

Exercise 5.4(c) Verbals as Direct Objects

Each of the following sentences from Alice Walker's novel *Possessing the Secret of Joy* contains a verbal as a direct object, either as an infinitive phrase or a participle phrase. Find the verbal, underline it, and then put a double line under the verb or verb phrase to which it serves as object. In the space below the sentence, write whether the verbal is an infinitive phrase or a participle phrase.

1. I began to paint fearsome birds.

2. She tried to laugh the whole thing off.

3. We had decided to go back to the village.

4. Your wife refuses to talk about her dreams.

5. I would enjoy hearing your wise words.

6. Evelyn tends to leave therapists prostrate in her wake.

7. My mother began to tell me the story of how she met my father.

8. We enjoyed watching the men and women who came out of their homes promptly at quarter to four.

9. I try to imagine a leopard on the path between our farm and the village.

10. She stopped weeping.

Exercise 5.5(a) Verbals as Subjects and Direct Objects

Underline the verbal in these sentences from *The House of the Spirits* and, in the space below the sentence, write the function of the phrase in the sentence (subject or direct object) and give the verb or verb phrase to which it relates as subject or object.

1. The child had stopped talking.

2. She must learn to love this land.

3. It would not be easy to send him away.

4. You'll learn to know each stone and each animal.

5. She failed to recognize the young man with the cruel eyes of a rodent.

6. It was better to spend his extra money on food for the hungry.

7. She tried placing her in a school run by Spanish nuns.

8. It took almost two years to complete the mausoleum.

9. García managed to make his plea.

10. He began to set Esteban's bones.

Exercise 5.5 (b) Verbals as Subjects and Direct Objects

Underline the verbal in these sentences from *Sole Survivor* and, in the space below the sentence, write the function of the phrase in the sentence (subject or direct object) and give the verb or verb phrase to which it relates as subject or object. Some sentences may have more than one verbal.

1.   They wanted to be certain.

2.   Knowing more details can't ever help you.

3.   She tried to ask who he was.

4.   They were not going to pinch her nose shut.

5.   She continued to seek the truth.

6.   Joe decided to reserve the rest of his story until he heard theirs.

7.   They will try to find her as soon as possible.

8.   Rosie desperately needed to talk to a reporter.

9.   Being aboard Flight 353 would have been like the middle of a bomb blast.

10.   She agreed to cooperate with them.

Exercise 5.5 (c) Verbals as Subjects and Direct Objects

Underline the verbal in these sentences from *Possessing the Secret of Joy* and, in the space below the sentence, write the function of the phrase in the sentence (subject or direct object) and give the verb or verb phrase to which it relates as subject or object. Some sentences may have more than one verbal.

1. M'Lissa had stopped showing any signs of death.

2. I had tried to live through Josh's body.

3. To meet them in tears is bad luck to us.

4. Tashi wants to wear a red dress.

5. It is possible to recognize the little figure from M'Lissa's hut.

6. You keep asking about events of your own time.

7. Have I stopped hating him?

8. Pierre began to speak in a gibberish of French.

9. To glimpse an ice cream vendor in one of the stations amused me.

10. She tried to know me.

Exercise 5.6(a) Participle Phrases as Objects of Prepositions

Each of the following sentences from *The House of the Spirits* has a participle phrase that is the object of a preposition. Underline the participle and then put a double line under the preposition for which it is the object.

1. I had got into the habit of typing all my letters to her.

2. The idea of becoming a deputy was a long-cherished dream of Severo's.

3. I was afraid of being rejected.

4. She was incapable of understanding any joke.

5. Trueba still owed him the reward for betraying Pedro Tercero García.

6. I felt capable of becoming a rich man.

7. She was far from knowing each of them by name.

8. My sister Férula helped me get closer to the del Valle family by uncovering distant links between our ancestors and theirs.

9. By that point I was used to having dead-end relationships.

10. I'm not trying to justify my sins by saying that I couldn't control my instincts.

Exercise 5.6 (b) Participle Phrases as Objects of Prepositions

Each of the following sentences from *Sole Survivor* has a participle phrase that is the object of a preposition. Underline the participle and then put a double line under the preposition for which it is the object.

1. After fetching an icy bottle of beer, Joe returned to the mattress.

2. She would have concentrated on comforting them.

3. Some days the planet turned twenty-four hours without rotating Joe.

4. He was trying to be one of them by matching their enthusiasm.

5. He had lost his way after losing his family.

6. The prospect of saving a life pushed Joe forward.

7. Nina had a way of crinkling her sweet face in pure delight at the sight of a dog or cat.

8. After selling the house in Studio City, he had brought no furniture with him.

9. Lisa thought about her answer before giving it.

10. He was unable to look upon a victim of a drive-by shooting without seeing Michelle or Chrissie or Nina.

Exercise 5.6(c) Participle Phrases as Objects of Prepositions

Each of the following sentences from *Possessing the Secret of Joy* has a participle phrase that is the object of a preposition. Underline the participle and then put a double line under the preposition for which it is the object.

1. I remember his shock at being constantly harassed.

2. We were intent on reaching the end of our long journey.

3. After being brought into the sunlight of her new home, a remarkable change had occurred.

4. I felt no compunction about opening letters that came from Lisette to Adam.

5. This nightmare of being held captive was what kept my father away from me.

6. Are they afraid of corrupting the young?

7. His words, on touching my ear, bounce back into his mouth.

8. Man's life was not capable of supporting both beings.

9. Pierre refrains from observing the situation out loud.

10. Did you not make a point of buying several razors?

Pulling Ideas Together

Exercise 6.1(a) Coordination

Circle the conjunction in each of the following sentences from *Robinson Crusoe* by Daniel Defoe. Then underline what the conjunction connects. Remember that the sentence parts connected by conjunctions must be equal. In the space below, note the kind of sentence parts that are connected (words, phrases, or clauses).

1.   I left my father and mother.

2.   I swam very well, yet I could not deliver myself from the waves.

3.   We sat looking upon one another and expecting death.

4.   I never saw them, or any sign of them.

5.   I found a large tortoise or turtle.

6.   Our case was dismal, for we saw that the boat could not live.

7.   I could feel myself carried with a mighty force and swiftness towards the shore.

8.   I resolved to get to the ship, so I took to the water.

9.   I first laid all the planks or boards upon it that I could get.

10.   I went to the bread-room and filled my pockets with biscuits.

Exercise 6.1 (b) Coordination

Circle the conjunction in each of the following sentences from *The Labyrinth of Solitude* by Octavio Paz. Then underline what the conjunction connects. Remember that the sentence parts connected by conjunctions must be equal. In the space below, note the kind of sentence parts that are connected (words, phrases, or clauses).

1. A sense of inferiority may sometimes be an illusion, but solitude is a hard fact.

2. He cannot recognize himself in his inhuman objects, nor in his fellows.

3. He has built his own world, and it is built in his image.

4. They are rich, and we are poor.

5. When I arrived in the United States, I was surprised by the self-assurance and confidence of the people.

6. They left the social or cultural structures intact.

7. Love is a hunger for life and a longing for death.

8. The North Americans are credulous, and we are believers.

9. He cannot grow or mature.

10. Our response to sympathy and tenderness is reserve.

Exercise 6.1(c) Coordination

Circle the conjunction in each of the following sentences from *Siddhartha* by Herman Hesse. Then underline what the conjunction connects. Remember that the sentence parts connected by conjunctions must be equal. In the space below, note the kind of sentence parts that are connected (words, phrases, or clauses).

1. The flesh disappeared from his legs and cheeks.

2. The sun or moon shone.

3. He returns from the illusion and finds everything as it was before.

4. Anyone can embrace or reject opinions.

5. On the evening of that day, they overtook the Samanas and requested their company.

6. The world was full of suffering, but the path to the release from suffering had been found.

7. Many wonderful and incredible things were reported about him.

8. They sat under the trees, lost in meditation or engaged in spirited talk.

9. He is sixty years old and has not attained Nirvana.

10. A heron flew over the bamboo wood, and Siddhartha took the heron into his soul.

Exercise 6.2 (a) Coordination

The following sentences come from *Robinson Crusoe*. Examine the conjunction used in each sentence; then insert commas where they are needed (I have removed all the commas that may be required by coordination). If a sentence is correct as it is, write *correct* under the sentence.

1. I learned to look more upon the bright side of my condition and less upon the dark side.

2. My next design was to make a tour round the island for I was very eager to see other parts of the coast.

3. I went away and was no more sad.

4. I cannot say any extraordinary thing happened to me but I lived on in the same course.

5. I might have raised shiploadings of corn but I had no use for it.

6. I made little lockers to put provisions necessaries and ammunition.

7. I saved the skins of all the creatures that I killed and I had hung them up, stretched out with sticks in the sun.

8. There was no wind stirring to help me and all I could do with my paddles signified nothing.

9. We never see the true state of our condition nor know how to value what we enjoy.

10. I went on shore to look about me and see where I was.

Exercise 6.2 (b) Coordination

The following sentences come from *The Labyrinth of Solitude*. Examine the conjunction used in each sentence; then insert commas where they are needed (I have removed all the commas that may be required by coordination). If a sentence is correct as it is, write *correct* under the sentence.

1. It would be a history of Mexican ideas but our history is only a fragment of world history.

2. The Revolution began as a discovery of our own selves and a return to our origins.

3. Zea has studied American alienation but it is now a condition shared by all men.

4. The Revolution has not succeeded in changing our country into a community or even in offering any hope of doing so.

5. The Independence movement the Reform movement and the Díaz dictatorship were distinct phases of one continuing effort to break free.

6. Their political economic and technical transformations seemed to be inspired by some superior coherency.

7. The first job was to recover and divide up the land.

8. The studies by Leopoldo Zea and Edmundo O'Gorman are especially important.

9. Our gains have to be defended constantly but at least the feudal regime has disappeared.

10. We did not even own the oil minerals electric power and other resources.

Exercise 6.2(c) Coordination

The following sentences come from *Siddhartha*. Examine the conjunction used in each sentence; then insert commas where they are needed (I have removed all the commas that may be required by coordination). If a sentence is correct as it is, write *correct* under the sentence.

1. Siddhartha looked up and around him.

2. The world was beautiful strange and mysterious.

3. Meaning and reality were not hidden somewhere behind things.

4. He was overwhelmed by a feeling of icy despair but he was more firmly himself than ever.

5. Siddhartha learned something new on every step of his path for the world was transformed.

6. He saw and recognized the visible.

7. The body was certainly not the Self nor the play of senses.

8. He felt the urge to enter the grove immediately but he thought it over.

9. He surveyed the town wandered about the maze of streets stood still in places and rested on the stone steps to the river.

10. She raised her head and looked at him.

Exercise 6.3(a) Correlative Conjunctions

Find the correlative conjunction pair in each of the following sentences from *Ethan Frome* by Edith Wharton, put a circle around each half of the pair, and then underline the two connected words, phrases, or clauses. (Other conjunctions also appear; for this exercise, focus only on correlative conjunctions.) In the space below, describe as accurately as possible the kinds of elements that are connected (for example, noun phrases, prepositional phrases, adjectives).

1. I have neither the time nor the energy right now.

2. I was getting to know him too well to express either wonder or gratitude at his keeping his appointment.

3. The sudden heat of his tone made her color mount again, not with a rush, but gradually.

4. He was struck by a new note in her voice. It was neither whiny nor reproachful.

5. With every yard of the way, some spot where they had stood both clutched at Ethan and dragged him back.

6. Neither poverty nor physical suffering could have put the expression there.

7. His loneliness was not the result of his personal plight, but the accumulated cold of many winters.

8. He regretted his words, not only because they were untrue, but also because he knew the imprudence of letting Zeena think he had funds.

9. Either it was the inevitable effect of life on the farm, or it was because Ethan never listened.

10. Most people were either indifferent to his troubles or disposed to thinking they were natural for a young fellow of his age.

Exercise 6.3 (b) Correlative Conjunctions

Find the correlative conjunction pair in each of the following sentences from *Siddhartha*, put a circle around each half of the pair, and then underline the two connected words, phrases, or clauses. (Other conjunctions also appear; for this exercise, focus only on correlative conjunctions.) In the space below, describe as accurately as possible the kinds of elements that are connected (for example, noun phrases, prepositional phrases, adjectives).

1. I will win him with both love and patience.

2. I did not hurt either myself or others.

3. Siddhartha neither ate meat nor drank wine.

4. He saw people living in a childish or animal-like way, which he both loved and despised.

5. Now I know it not only with my intellect but with my heart.

6. They listened silently to the water, which to them was not just water but the voice of life.

7. You have both heard the bird in your breast sing and followed it.

8. They found neither magicians nor wise men.

9. Either the boy had long ago left the wood, or he was hiding from his pursuer.

10. Within you there is both a stillness and a sanctuary.

Exercise 6.3(c) Correlative Conjunctions

Find the correlative conjunction pair in each of the following sentences from *The Labyrinth of Solitude*, put a circle around each half of the pair, and then underline the two connected words, phrases, or clauses. (Other conjunctions also appear; for this exercise, focus only on correlative conjunctions.) In the space below, describe as accurately as possible the kinds of elements that are connected (for example, noun phrases, prepositional phrases, adjectives).

1. Neither the Mexican nor the North American has achieved this reconciliation.

2. They are not the result of other events, but the result of a single will.

3. The battle cry is both a challenge and an affirmation.

4. To the Mexican there are only two possibilities in life: either he inflicts actions on others, or he suffers them himself at the hands of others.

5. We are enigmatic not only to strangers but also to ourselves.

6. The phrase is said not to protect another, but to impose one's superiority.

7. A historical event is not the sum of its component factors but an indissoluble reality.

8. The cult of the Virgin reflects a concrete historical situation in both the spiritual realm and the material realm.

9. The Virgin's principal attribute is not to watch over the fertility of the earth but to provide refuge for the unfortunate.

10. Not only does this essay extend the book and bring it up to date, but it is also a new attempt to decipher reality.

Exercise 6.4 (a) Conjunctive Adverbs and Adverbials

Circle the conjunctive adverb or adverbial in each of the following passages from *In the Absence of the Sacred* by Jerry Mander. In the space below the sentence, write the meaning relationship it indicates.

1. In those days TV had the quality of movie-going. Soon, however, each family had its own set.

2. I heard Reagan use the same style and many of the same words from the commercial imagery of the post–World War II period. In fact, Reagan's success may be explained in part by his connection to that optimistic time.

3. People who celebrate technology say it has brought us an improved standard of living. In addition, it has brought the contributions of modern medicine.

4. The camp was sports-oriented. One period per week, however, we had what was called "nature."

5. Modern medicine has improved life expectancy. On the other hand, critics argue that it may be a two-edged sword.

6. In giving trust to media imagery, we are like the deer staring at the headlight. Likewise, we assume that by observing a machine's performance personally we can understand its full implications.

7. There is an appeal in the existence of machines that have such promise. Moreover, the new machines actually do what they promise to do.

8. Nuclear technology steers society toward greater political and financial centralization. Solar energy, on the other hand, is biased toward democratic use.

9. Technological innovation was good, invariably good. Fifty years later, however, we are at an appropriate moment to question this path we have chosen.

10. So it becomes okay to humiliate any way of thinking that stands in the way of a kind of "progress" we have invented. In fact, it becomes more than acceptable for us to bulldoze nature and native societies.

Exercise 6.4 (b) Conjunctive Adverbs and Adverbials

Circle the conjunctive adverb or adverbial in each of the following passages from *The Bow and the Lyre* by Octavio Paz. In the space below the sentence, write the meaning relationship it indicates.

1. The reader reproduces the poet's actions and experiences. Moreover, almost all periods of crisis or social decadence are fertile in great poets.

2. Both directions express man's revolt against his own condition. Thus, "to change man" means to renounce being a man.

3. The poem is an attempt to transcend language; on the other hand, poetic expressions exist on the same plane as speech.

4. The poem will continue to be one of the few resources by which man can go beyond himself. Therefore, the spark of the poetic cannot be confused with the more decisive endeavors of poetry.

5. Poems gave European nations consciousness of themselves. Indeed, by means of poetry, the common language was changed into mythical images.

6. The propagandist's task is to transmit certain directives from the higher to the lower level. The poet, on the other hand, works from the lower to the higher level.

7. A society's fatigue does not necessarily imply the extinction of the arts. Instead, it may have the opposite effect.

8. The poem is a living whole, made of irreplaceable elements. Thus, the true translation can only be a re-creation.

9. Rhythm is meaning and it says "something." Thus, its verbal or ideological content is not separable.

10. Death completes human life. Therefore, to live is to face death.

Exercise 6.4 (c) Conjunctive Adverbs and Adverbials

Circle the conjunctive adverb or adverbial in each of the following passages from *The Seven Storey Mountain* by Thomas Merton. In the space below the sentence, write the meaning relationship it indicates.

1. They sent my uncle and John Paul to choir school. Indeed, there was talk of sending me there.

2. He did shave his beard off. However, he had something to tell me that upset my complacency far more than the beard.

3. Father could not leave the training and care of his sons to other people. Moreover, he had become definitely aware of certain religious obligations.

4. The school consisted of a big, clean, white building overlooking the river. However, there was something about it that Father did not like.

5. Father was by no means in love with French Protestantism. In fact, there had been not a little likelihood that he might become a Catholic.

6. We traveled all over the countryside looking at places to build a house. Thus, I was constantly in and out of old churches.

7. Father was English; therefore, the rugby club assumed he was an expert in every type of sport.

8. Father occasionally refereed their wild games, at the risk of his life. However, he lived through the season.

9. We could not judge what the old church had been like. Even now, however, the rebuilt church dominated the town.

10. I wanted to be in all those places which the pictures showed me. Indeed, it was a kind of problem that I could not be in all of them at once.

Exercise 6.5 (a) Conjunctive Adverbs and Adverbials

The following sentences from *In the Absence of the Sacred* contain conjunctions joining clauses. Rewrite each sentence so that you convert these conjunctions into conjunctive adverbs or adverbials and change the punctuation to make it appropriate. Be sure to pick an adverb or adverbial that conveys a meaning similar to that of the original conjunction. If no conjunctive adverb is similar enough in meaning to the conjunction, use a semicolon.

1. This highway is the only road out of the capital city, but it is actually little more than a bulldozed dirt track.

2. More dog teams were tied up nearby, and many of the houses had rifles outside.

3. There's no way my children could grow up as Indians in New York, and there's no way I'm going back to Haiti.

4. Some of the students were in their early twenties, but most were in their late teens.

5. Some came from communities where there hadn't been schools, and others just hadn't attended the schools.

6. Most of the houses were built with stripped logs, but tarpaper houses were not unusual.

7. You dress and behave according to corporate concepts, and you interact with the machines by which corporations accomplish their tasks.

8. Laraque was born in Haiti, but she identifies most strongly with her Indian heritage.

9. Mr. Anderson was quoted as saying that he had "overreacted," and he was now prepared to lead the company in its legal fight.

10. We had been talking for about five minutes, but there were already signs of restlessness in the room.

Exercise 6.5 (b) Conjunctive Adverbs and Adverbials

The following sentences from *The Bow and the Lyre* contain conjunctions joining clauses. Rewrite each sentence so that you convert these conjunctions into conjunctive adverbs or adverbials and change the punctuation to make it appropriate. Be sure to pick an adverb or adverbial that conveys a meaning similar to that of the original conjunction. If no conjunctive adverb is similar enough in meaning to the conjunction, use a semicolon.

1. A minute ago we were settled in our world, and we moved about naturally.

2. The poem's images do not lead us to something else, but they bring us face to face with a concrete reality.

3. Language goes beyond the circle of relative meanings, and it says the unsayable.

4. A landscape by Góngora is not the same as a natural landscape, but both possess reality and consistency.

5. Poetry puts man outside himself, and it simultaneously makes him return to his original being.

6. The image reconciles opposites, but this reconciliation cannot be explained by words.

7. The Lacandons live under really archaic conditions, but they are the direct descendants of the Mayas, whose civilization was the richest that flourished in the Americas.

8. We are speechless, and the rapture takes our breath away.

9. The poem does not allude to reality, but it tries to recreate it.

10. Paulo is guilty of not being able to hear, but God expresses himself as silence.

Exercise 6.5(c) Conjunctive Adverbs and Adverbials

The following sentences from *The Seven Storey Mountain* contain conjunctions joining clauses. Rewrite each sentence so that you convert these conjunctions into conjunctive adverbs or adverbials and change the punctuation to make it appropriate. Be sure to pick an adverb or adverbial that conveys a meaning similar to that of the original conjunction. If no conjunctive adverb is similar enough in meaning to the conjunction, use a semicolon.

1.   My veins were bursting with political enthusiasms, and I had signed up for courses in sociology.

2.   I went and changed everything with the registrar, so I remained in that class for the rest of the year.

3.   It was the best course I ever had at college, and it did me the most good.

4.   I did not graduate in June, but I nominally belonged to that year's class.

5.   I would now be a teacher, and I would live the rest of my life in the relative peace of a college campus.

6.   Gibney was interested in philosophy, but he did not have enough interest to bring about any kind of a conversion.

7.   I have forgotten the titles, even the authors, and I never understood a word of what they said in the first place.

8.   Lax was born with the deepest sense of who God was, but he would not make a move without the others.

9.   I had the habit of reading fast, and all these mysteries would require a great deal of thought.

10. Blake has done his work for me, and he did it very thoroughly.

CHAPTER SEVEN

Agreement

Exercise 7.1(a) Subject–Verb Agreement

The verb of each of the following sentences from *The Portrait of a Lady* by Henry James has been omitted. In the space provided, write the correct form of the verb given in brackets.

1. He _____ me a list. [past tense of *give*]

2. It _____ a great many rare and valuable books. [present tense of *contain*]

3. I _____ who some of them were. [past tense of *ask*]

4. Ralph _____ well enough. [present tense of *understand*]

5. He _____ me they were people who at various times seemed to like him. [past tense of *tell*]

6. She _____ one of the rare and valuable volumes. [past tense of *find*]

7. I _____ he is an old friend of yours. [present tense of *know*]

8. Her eyes often _____ from the book in her hand to the open window. [past tense of *wander*]

9. She _____ a modest vehicle approach the door. [past tense of *see*]

10. The theory _____ her little rest. [past tense of *bring*]

Exercise 7.1(b) Subject–Verb Agreement

The verb of each of the following sentences from *The Bow and the Lyre* has been omitted. In the space provided, write the correct form of the verb given in brackets.

1. One _____ the leap and tries to reach the shore. [present tense of *take*]

2. Saint John of the Cross _____ he was serving his faith with his poems. [past tense of *believe*]

3. Technology _____ between us and the world. [present tense of *come*]

4. In the Asiatic colonies, the religion of the gods _____ stronger. [past tense of *grow*]

5. Poetry always _____ on something alien to it. [present tense of *lean*]

6. The poem _____ beyond words and history. [present tense of *go*]

7. Immigration to Asia Minor _____ a religion of heroes. [past tense of *bring*]

8. Poetry _____ to escape from history's law of gravity. [present tense of *seem*]

9. They all _____ themselves as being apart from society. [present tense of *regard*]

10. The poetic word _____ a social product. [present tense of *constitute*]

Exercise 7.1(c) Subject–Verb Agreement

The verb of each of the following sentences from *Joseph in Egypt* has been omitted. In the space provided, write the correct form of the verb given in brackets.

1. The tree _____ its shade. [present tense of *spread*]

2. Laban _____ to the primitive. [present tense of *cling*]

3. Such things _____ to pass now and then in the world. [present tense of *come*]

4. Your name _____ another meaning. [present tense of *have*]

5. I _____ not the truth. [past tense of *speak*]

6. I only _____ these things to be gruff. [past tense of *say*]

7. Joseph _____ passed through the little gate [past tense of *have*]

8. The orchard _____ from the east edge of the pond. [past tense of *continue*]

9. Joseph _____ the steps. [past tense of *mount*]

10. The tradition _____ such stories. [past tense of *lack*]

Exercise 7.2 (a) The Verb <u>Be</u>

Each of the following sentences from *The Fountainhead* by Ayn Rand contains a form of the verb *be*. Underline it, describe it as an auxiliary or a main verb, and give its tense (present or past), its number (singular or plural), and, if it is present-tense singular, its person.

1.   He was crossing the porch without noticing her.

2.   I am so sorry about what happened this morning.

3.   Petey is graduating today.

4.   We are all in our rightful place.

5.   It was a large, bare room.

6.   Mallory was sent to jail to await trial.

7.   "Mr. Roark!" she gasped, "You are not going like this?"

8.   We weren't talking about you.

9.   I am speaking of your attitude toward the subject.

10.   The great style of the Renaissance is far from dead.

Exercise 7.2(b) The Verb <u>Be</u>

Each of the following sentences from *Kerouac* by Ann Charters contains a form of the verb *be*. Underline it, describe it as an auxiliary or a main verb, and give its tense (present or past), its number (singular or plural), and, if it is present-tense singular, its person.

1. Kerouac was sleeping in Edie's apartment.

2. His parents were less angry with him.

3. Pie and ice cream are practically all I ate.

4. The book is full of these crazy poems.

5. Neal was acting like an irresponsible kid.

6. I am in the West.

7. Lucien was ready to turn himself in.

8. You are rocking the boat back there!

9. The roof is slippery.

10. They were heading for Los Angeles.

Exercise 7.2(c) The Verb <u>Be</u>

Each of the following sentences from *The Tenants of Time* by Thomas Flanagan contains a form of the verb *be*. Underline it, describe it as an auxiliary or a main verb, and give its tense (present or past), its number (singular or plural), and, if it is present-tense singular, its person.

1. McMahon himself was history.

2. His mother and my father were brother and sister.

3. The treatment of Irish prisoners is difficult to accept.

4. I am certain that he drank alone.

5. Bob was drinking a bit more than he should.

6. Their house is hidden by the bend.

7. The celebrated gardens were laid out after a formal design by Cassels.

8. The effect is pleasing.

9. You are most welcome.

10. The song is his memorial.

Exercise 7.3 (a) Subject–Verb Agreement

Underline the correct verb form in the parentheses for each of the following. These sentences are taken from *The Fountainhead*.

1. There (is, are) someone here who seems to be ignoring you.

2. It (was, were) strange to see a face presenting no meaning.

3. Roark and Dominique (was, were) left alone.

4. So Joel talked about badminton; that (was, were) his hobby.

5. There (was, were) no expression on her face.

6. The expression of his eyes (has, have) to be heard, not seen: it is a visual roar of laughter.

7. It (was, were) interesting to discover what sort of thing appears good-looking to you.

8. Dominique and I (am, are) always kidding each other.

9. There (is, are) nothing as significant as a human face.

10. It (was, were) almost indecent to see them together.

Exercise 7.3 (b) Subject–Verb Agreement

Underline the correct verb form in the parentheses for each of the following. These sentences are taken from *Kerouac*.

1.   The others sitting in the front seat of the car (was, were) on the wrong path.

2.   Everyone (was, were) relieved to end the chaotic association.

3.   Renouncing Neal (was, were) part of clearing up the loose ends of his past.

4.   Something (was, were) happening to him that he didn't understand.

5.   There (was, were) strong best-sellers out at the same time.

6.   All the available jobs (was, were) given to more experienced seamen.

7.   His careening rush over the roads of Nevada and Utah (was, were) too much for the other passengers.

8.   All I hope (is, are) that someday we'll be able to live on the same street.

9.   There (was, were) angry scenes between her and Kerouac.

10. When he and Joan (was, were) married, his mother had moved out of their old apartment.

Exercise 7.3 (c) Subject–Verb Agreement

Underline the correct verb form in the parentheses for each of the following. These sentences are taken from *The Tenants of Time*.

1. The front windows of the house (was, were) lit.

2. There (is, are) so many Irishmen in Chicago that you can lose yourself among them.

3. I went up to Dublin to pay a visit upon Bob Delaney, who (was, were) in Dublin upon Land League business.

4. "Small blame," they would say, "after the things that (was, were) done to him in that prison."

5. It (is, are) painful now to look back on those years.

6. Everything (seem, seems) to be happening at once.

7. There (was, were) no gas lights.

8. Each of them in turn (comes, come) forward to say that Parnell was simply "Parnell" to him, but "Mr. Parnell" to others.

9. It (was, were) like early winter, that summer of `seventy-eight.

10. There (was, were) no ballad hawkers outside Kilmainham.

Exercise 7.4 (a) Pronoun–Antecedent Agreement

In the following sentences from *The Bow and the Lyre*, Octavio Paz uses the masculine pronoun and the noun *man* to represent all of humankind. In addition, the masculine pronoun is used to replace the noun *poet*. First, underline every pronoun you find and circle its antecedent. Then rewrite each sentence so that it no longer uses the masculine pronoun for generic reference. (Hint: One trick is to make the noun phrase plural by using such words as "people" or "human beings." Sometimes, however, this strategy won't work. Try to be creative, but remember to make verbs agree with their subjects.)

1. Both directions express man's revolt against his own condition.

2. The poem will continue to be one of the few resources by which man can go beyond himself.

3. Poetry puts man outside himself and it simultaneously makes him return to his original being.

4. The words of the poet, precisely because they are words, are his and others'.

5. The middle class exiles the poet and transforms him into a parasite or a vagabond.

6. The poet does not see in his images the revelation of a strange power.

7. Moved by the need to ground his activity, the poet doubles as critic.

8. The modern poet will occupy his former place, usurped by the priest.

9. By means of imagination man states his infinite desire.

10. Man is language because he is the one who speaks and the one who listens.

© 1998 NTC/Contemporary Publishing Co.

Exercise 7.4 (b) Pronoun–Antecedent Agreement

In the following sentences from *On the Nature of the Universe*, Lucretius uses the masculine pronoun and the noun *man* to represent all of humankind. First, underline every pronoun you find and circle its antecedent. Then rewrite each sentence so that it no longer uses the masculine pronoun for generic reference. (Hint: One trick is to make the noun phrase plural by using such words as "people" or "human beings." Sometimes, however, this strategy won't work. Try to be creative, but remember to make verbs agree with their subjects.)

1. Look at a man in the midst of doubt and danger, and you will learn in his hour of adversity what he is really like.

2. At the instant when a man is mastered by death, you cannot tell that any part of the whole has been fetched away from his body.

3. It was nature that drove man to utter his words.

4. When the pervasive power of wine has entered into a man, his limbs are overcome by heaviness, his speech is slurred, and all the other symptoms follow in due order.

5. It may happen that a man is seized with a sudden spasm of epilepsy; he falls as though struck and foams at the mouth.

6. We often see a man pass away little by little, and lose his vital sensibility limb by limb.

7. But suppose it is a man of riper years who complains at his approaching end.

8. No man on the point of death seems to feel his spirit retiring intact right out of his body.

9. With what is left of his body a man presses on with battle and bloodshed.

10. A mere jolt out of sleep enables a man to pull himself together.

Exercise 7.4 (c) Pronoun-Antecedent Agreement

In the following sentences from *The Labyrinth of Solitude*, Octavio Paz uses the masculine pronoun in reference to Mexican people and people of other nationalities. First, underline every pronoun you find and circle its antecedent. Then rewrite each sentence so that it no longer uses the masculine pronoun for generic reference. (Hint: Try simply making the noun phrase plural. Remember to make verbs agree with their subjects.)

1. To the Mexican there are only two possibilities in life: either he inflicts actions on others, or he suffers them himself at the hands of others.

2. The Mexican also strives to be formal in his daily life.

3. The Mexican does not open himself up to the outside world.

4. While the Mexican tries to create closed worlds in his politics and in the arts, he wants modesty, prudence, and a ceremonious reserve to rule over his everyday life.

5. The North American hides or denies certain parts of his body and, more often, of his psyche.

6. How could a poor Mexican live without two or three annual fiestas that make up for his poverty and misery?

7. The Mexican tells us that human beings are a mixture; he uses analysis rather than synthesis.

8. The Mexican is a good deal more pagan than the Spaniard, and he does not condemn the natural world.

9. During these days the silent Mexican whistles, shouts, sings, shoots off fireworks, and discharges his pistol into the air.

10. The Mexican is horrified by appearances, though his leaders profess to love them.

Punctuation

Exercise 8.1(a) Sentence–Final Punctuation

Each of the following sentences from *The Fountainhead* lacks a sentence-final punctuation mark. Put a period, a question mark, or an exclamation point at the end of each sentence.

1. Why did I choose Howard Roark

2. He shrugged and settled back in his chair

3. Roark waved his privilege to make an opening statement to the jury

4. What can you tell us about Mr. Roark's career

5. I want an audience

6. I don't see what's so wrong with trying to please people

7. In the next two days a succession of witnesses testified for the plaintiff

8. It's a business like any other, isn't it

9. I always wanted to be honest with myself, but I'm not

10. Why are you all afraid of him

Exercise 8.1 (b) Sentence-Final Punctuation

Each of the following sentences from *Kerouac* lacks a sentence-final punctuation mark. Put a period, a question mark, or an exclamation point at the end of each sentence.

1. Cowley asked him to keep writing about his friends

2. Kerouac made himself the spokesman for his friends' ideas

3. Is there a beat generation

4. What am I going to do tomorrow

5. There were always drunken musicians with him

6. He felt a little uncomfortable about the lapse of time between completed novels

7. Who understands these things

8. What am I doing here

9. He wondered whether or not Neal wanted to talk to him

10. Is this the way I'm supposed to feel

Exercise 8.1(c) Sentence–Final Punctuation

Each of the following sentences from *The Tenants of Time* lacks a sentence-final punctuation mark. Put a period, a question mark, or an exclamation point at the end of each sentence.

1. When he reads, his lips move silently

2. What am I saying

3. I am ashamed of you

4. Where did Tobin find the money to take up the lease

5. We have no notion of what a season or two of ruined harvests means to these people

6. He will at least be snug and warm in prison

7. You know that song, do you not

8. Hound a man into the grave and then name a street after him. What a country

9. The granite boulder was your notion, was it not

10. Is any place as fine as Connemara

Exercise 8.2(a) Punctuation Inside the Sentence

Some of these sentences from Theodora Kroeber's *Ishi, Last of His Tribe* are correct as is; some have missing punctuation. Add punctuation where it is needed; write *correct* under the sentences that need no changes.

1. Ishi examined each tree choosing at last a branch for his new bow.

2. It was straight and strong the wood was not too young or too old.

3. Their only tools were stone and obsidian rasps.

4. Jikula did not forget that he awaited his chance for revenge.

5. Tushi cannot dig the heavy pine roots and she cannot carry everything Mother and Grandmother want.

6. We did it with only such sounds as the rubbing and snapping the wind make.

7. He found no footprints no smell and no sound of white men.

8. Tushi could not keep from laughing thinking of Ishi traveling like a mole.

9. Quail rabbits deer and the red fox melted into the brush.

10. Their long hair streamed behind them their quivers thumped against their backs.

Exercise 8.2 (b) *Punctuation Inside the Sentence*

Some of these sentences from James Michener's *Chesapeake* are correct as is; some have missing punctuation. Add punctuation where it is needed; write *correct* under the sentences that need no changes.

1. Both sons and daughters had married conservatively and no scandal had ever touched the family.

2. Cardinal Wolsey sent a personal emissary young Hugh Latimer with an argument that could not be refuted.

3. He neither solicited nor expected anything in return.

4. Satisfied as to the facts Devon Steed led the western counties in their support of the divorce.

5. Furthermore she gleefully executed Lutherans.

6. He arrived one Friday and told Sir Latimer he wanted to conduct Mass for Catholics in the area.

7. Edmund worked for the government in London and was invited by his associates to their places in the country.

8. It was understandable therefore that devout English priests were filtered into England to protect the faith.

9. He was a philosopher a historian an author and a superb theologian.

10. He remembered the place with affection low towers innumerable chimneys and four noble Gothic arches.

Exercise 8.2(c) Punctuation Inside the Sentence

Some of these sentences from M. Scott Peck's *The Road Less Traveled* are correct as is; some have missing punctuation. Add punctuation where it is needed; write *correct* under the sentences that need no changes.

1. I knew six weeks ago that I was running through my money fast but somehow I couldn't believe that it would come to this point.

2. Therefore it is up to other people or society to solve this problem for me.

3. My fellow residents and I were assigned new patients on rotation.

4. My friend will speak of the oppressive forces in our society racism sexism the military-industrial establishment and the country police who pick on him.

5. I was free to choose not to work so hard and to structure my time differently.

6. He described his childhood as normal and his parents as average.

7. Millions and even billions attempt daily to escape from freedom.

8. In the past in American culture contemplation has not been held in high regard.

9. Character-disordered people however make disastrous parents.

10. Thus two siblings fighting will always blame each other for the fight.

Exercise 8.3(a) The Apostrophe

Each of the following sentences from *Ishi, Last of His Tribe* has at least one word that requires an apostrophe. Underline that word, and rewrite it in the space below, inserting the apostrophe where it is needed. Be careful not to mistake ordinary plurals for possessive forms.

1. Tears ran down Elder Uncles face.

2. There will be again the empty cave, Grizzly Bears Hiding Place.

3. Ishi took his bow to the hollow where he cried alone, thinking of Tushis and Mothers tears.

4. There is much I didnt see.

5. They sat looking to the west, Grandfather holding Grandmothers little claw of a hand.

6. They grab each others right hands.

7. My dream is never the same, but my dreams road is surely the Suns road.

8. The museum men dont press in upon me.

9. The sky world danced over Ishis head.

10. Its not you or Tushi who need me now.

Exercise 8.3 (b) The Apostrophe

Each of the following sentences from *Chesapeake* has at least one word that requires an apostrophe. Underline that word, and rewrite it in the space below, inserting the apostrophe where it is needed. Be careful not to mistake ordinary plurals for possessive forms.

1.   Hes like an animal; that is for certain.

2.   It was a pleasant sail to Saint Marys City.

3.   Ive seen land twice as good as this.

4.   Ill take him off your hands.

5.   She arrived at her neighbors plantation well past dark.

6.   It was remarkable how quickly one became accustomed to Turlocks conversation.

7.   Its to be the other way around.

8.   Your father and I were often the objects of the laws persecution.

9.   Weve discussed his attack on Janney.

10.   Youre to be attentive and mind your manners.

Exercise 8.3(c) The Apostrophe

Each of the following sentences from *The Road Less Traveled* has at least one word that requires an apostrophe. Underline that word, and rewrite it in the space below, inserting the apostrophe where it is needed. Be careful not to mistake ordinary plurals for possessive forms.

1. All of lifes problems can be solved.

2. My mother loved me so much she wouldnt let me take the school bus.

3. John can defend himself; hes strong enough.

4. When a child is hungry, mother doesnt always appear to feed it.

5. Falling in love is not an extension of ones limits or boundaries.

6. I assumed she couldnt be the right person for me.

7. The essence of falling in love is a sudden collapse of a section of an individuals ego boundaries.

8. I didnt really love my husband when we were married.

9. We will be able to satisfy all of each others needs forever and ever.

10. She wants to go to the movies; he doesnt.

Exercise 8.4 (a) Punctuation in Direct Quotation

The following sentences from *Ishi, Last of His Tribe* involve direct quotation. I have left off some of the punctuation, including the quotation marks. Add punctuation where it is necessary.

1. In the office, Ishi asked How are these matters known?

2. I think they bring fresh salmon today Ishi said to him.

3. When it was finished, Ishi asked Could you tell the story of the old ones?

4. The shelves fill as do your notebooks Ishi sometimes said when Majapa came to sit on the wagon-cloth with him.

5. Majapa said It is time we go to Outer Ocean.

6. She said There is a family of skunks.

7. I want you to see she said to Ishi. They are so pretty.

8. Please sign here he said.

9. He called to Majapa Come, we fish!

10. This is very fine workmanship Majapa said. Where did you find it?

Exercise 8.4(b) Punctuation in Direct Quotation

The following sentences from *Chesapeake* involve direct quotation. I have left off some of the punctuation, including the quotation marks. Add punctuation where it is necessary.

1. Is your father home? he asked abruptly.

2. We'll give notice to the meeting on Sunday Starbuck said.

3. And now you may kiss her Micah said.

4. Bartley asked May I sit down?

5. It's Paxmore! they shouted.

6. Trying isn't good enough she instructed Rachel Watch over him.

7. We've heard you're a fine young man she said.

8. The child said I'll take him up the middle of the stream.

9. Herman Cline asked Where have you got him hidden?

10. I think he's in the woods over there Lafe said.

Exercise 8.4 (c) Punctuation in Direct Quotation

The following sentences from *The Road Less Traveled* involve direct quotation. I have left off some of the punctuation, including the quotation marks. Add punctuation where it is necessary.

1. I can't believe you really feel that way! Rachel exclaimed.

2. I can kick you out of here any time I want to I said.

3. What do you mean? I asked.

4. I cannot do it she said. I cannot let myself go.

5. Would you really do that? she asked.

6. I never knew what it was like to be relaxed with another person before she said.

7. Well she said last session you wanted me to cry.

8. I pointed out to Rachel that she always said Thank you.

9. What's wrong with being polite? she asked.

10. Look Rachel I said when I take on a case such as yours I make a commitment to that case.